HALF-HOURS WITH
WILLIAM HENDRIKSEN

HALF-HOURS
WITH
WILLIAM HENDRIKSEN

Stirring Devotional Surveys of
Romans, Philippians, Luke
and Revelation
with other gems

THE WAKEMAN TRUST, LONDON

HALF-HOURS WITH WILLIAM HENDRIKSEN
© Wakeman Trust 2007

Passages from Commentaries
© William Hendriksen
(used with permission of Banner of Truth Trust; www.banneroftruth.co.uk)

THE WAKEMAN TRUST
(Wakeman Trust is a UK Registered Charity)

UK Registered Office
38 Walcot Square
London SE11 4TZ

US Office
300 Artino Drive
Oberlin, OH 44074-1263
Website: www.wakemantrust.org

ISBN 978 1 870855 62 4

Cover design by Vera Sun

Printed by Stephens & George, Merthyr Tydfil, UK

Contents

Introduction by Dr Peter Masters

Tribute to William Hendriksen, 1900-1982   7

Part 1

1   Super-invincibility
    The Message of Romans   13

2   Trust, Try, Travel and Triumph
    A Survey of Philippians   27

3   Four Special Features
    of the Gospel of Luke   39

4   The Heavenly Jerusalem
    A Survey of Revelation   49

Part 2

    Great Passages from William Hendriksen
    drawn from his commentaries   63

'More than a Conqueror'
Tribute to William Hendriksen
1900 – 1982

DR HENDRIKSEN'S commentaries, covering thirteen New Testament books, have endeared him to numerous Bible students in all parts of the world. Few authors have combined such thoroughness and depth of scholarship with such warmth and simplicity of style. His commentary work reflected 28 years' experience in the preaching ministry – serving large Michigan pastorates – and nine years as Professor of New Testament at Calvin Theological Seminary, Grand Rapids.

Even in advancing years Dr Hendriksen never relaxed in his driving concern to be about his work. Throughout life he had been a prodigious worker, the sacrifices and experiences of his early years conspiring to forge and frame a man of tremendous feeling and self-discipline.

Born in the Netherlands in 1900, he was ten years old when his family emigrated to America, settling in Kalamazoo, Michigan. There, in years of depression and acute financial hardship, sub-zero winter temperatures could be bitterly cruel. His father was a craftsman woodcarver who had been obliged to turn his skills to mending clocks, sewing machines and virtually anything else, in order to support the family. Though he brought up his eight children to love the Gospel, he could not adjust to the romantic desire of William, the youngest, to become a minister, and so William Hendriksen left school at 14 to work in a grocer's shop. However, his determination to be a minister of the Gospel drove him to personal study, night school and correspondence courses, and at 18 he secured a job as a schoolteacher in Chicago. Later he became the schoolmaster of a one-classroom school in Iowa teaching children aged 5 to 13 all at the same time.

At 20 he was accepted for study at Calvin College, Grand Rapids, working his passage. Alongside his BA degree he studied science subjects, specialising in chemistry. On graduating he was offered an appointment as a Lecturer in Organic Chemistry by a professor who advised him against entering the ministry on account of his weak voice. (In later years the professor became an elder in Dr Hendriksen's congregation, describing him as the best preacher under whom he had ever sat.)

From Calvin College he proceeded into Calvin Theological Seminary where he became a prize-winning student under such giants as Professor Louis Berkhof. In those days a seminary student at Calvin Seminary was expected to learn the entire Greek Testament by heart and to recite any part of it on request.

In 1927 the aspiring preacher entered the ministry of the Christian Reformed Church, serving congregations in Zeeland, Muskegon and Grand Rapids. In each place he was used of God to build up the membership, his last congregation rising above 1,500.

In 1938 Dr Hendriksen gave a detailed series of studies in the *Book of Revelation* to a regular meeting of Christian businessmen in Grand Rapids, his hearers strongly urging him to publish the messages. In response he arranged a small private printing of *More Than Conquerors*. Very soon a new young publisher named Herman Baker bought the little stock to launch his publishing business. For both author and publisher it was the 'first book', and it continues in print today having passed through over 30 editions, and having given immense blessing to a vast number of readers around the world. Baker Book House became one of the world's largest evangelical publishing houses.

In 1943 Dr Hendriksen took the appointment of Professor of New Testament at Calvin Seminary, where he was a close colleague and friend of Professor Louis Berkhof. Among his academic honours was an earned doctorate in theology from Princeton Seminary.

William Hendriksen returned to pastoral ministry in 1952, and the following year the first volume of his *New Testament Commentary* appeared – the exposition of *John's Gospel*. After the death of his first wife, he married again in 1961, and for the remainder of his life he and Reta worked together on the commentary ministry.

At 65 he 'retired' to Florida to devote himself to these unique commentaries. He and his wife established a home free from luxurious excesses and dedicated themselves together to completing the task, Reta typing and retyping the text as it was produced.

The first stage of a commentary was always the translation of the text from the Greek. Then, making use of his multi-lingual capacities, Dr Hendriksen would sift the theological literature of Germany and Holland, along with English language works, before arriving at his conclusions. His disarming and unaffected style concealed considerable exegetical and comparative preparation.

In 1979 Dr Hendriksen visited Britain to be the special guest speaker at the Metropolitan Tabernacle School of Theology. Pastors and Christian workers were at once captivated by his bearing and feelingful delivery, each address constituting a lesson in communication – the art of taking sublime truths and helping people feel them in their hearts. Speaking personally, I shall not forget my visits to Dr Hendriksen's Florida home so many years ago. His humility and approachability were conspicuous, but his total preoccupation with the work of the Saviour was always the most striking of all. Taking Dr Hendriksen on a sightseeing drive round central London was an experience worth recalling. Significant places seldom evoked more than a polite inclination of the head, because conversation remained firmly riveted on church history or the Lord's work. It took the biblical exhibits of the British Museum to capture the expositor's enthusiasm for sightseeing.

Dr Hendriksen was deeply disturbed over the decline in doctrinal purity of once stalwart church groups and seminaries. Theologically, he never wavered from the 'old paths', and his strong sympathies were entirely with those who took a clear and uncompromising stand for the faith. His outstanding powers were gifts from the Lord, to Whom all praise is due, but we honour and admire the man for his stewardship of these gifts – for his total and unselfish devotion to his calling, his exhaustive toil, his refusal to be drawn into the world of 'scholarship' for its own sake, his loyalty to the reformed faith, and his undying love for evangelism.

We especially admire the example he set in all his written works (already mentioned) of combining quality of scholarship with simplicity of expression and application. This skill is to be seen in some classic extracts from his commentaries included in the last part of this book. May many readers be enlightened and encouraged through these pages from the lips and pen of an exceptional Bible commentator.

PETER MASTERS

Four Talks
at the Annual School of Theology
Metropolitan Tabernacle
1979*

Dr Hendriksen prefaced his first address
with this explanation

NOW IT HAS BEEN SAID that I am going to deliver four lectures. I just wish to correct that a moment. It is four *talks*. There is a difference you know between a lecture and a talk. When you give a talk, you use ordinary language which everybody can understand, such as when you say – two times two is four. That is a talk. But if you wish to convey the same idea – two times two is four – in lecture style, you would have to say the following:–

'When in the course of human events it becomes necessary or imperative that the cardinal of the second denomination rank or order functioning as a multiplicand, be placed in vertical or perpendicular relationship to its equal or counterpart operating as a multiplier, then come what may, do or die, sink or swim, survive or perish, the result, the product of the afore implied mathematical computation or calculation has ever been, is today and as long as suns continue, evermore will be four.'

So you know now what I mean when I say I will give talks. But even though they will be talks, the subjects are nevertheless tremendously important, and very comforting too.

---

* Delivered without notes, from memory, including all Scripture quotations and poems. Dr Hendriksen was in his eightieth year.

1
Super-invincibility
The Message of Romans

A S YOU KNOW, my dear friends, my wife and I are visitors here. By way of introduction I want to speak to you about another visitor, and let you guess for a while what visitor I have in mind. The particular visitor I am thinking about is quite old. A hundred years old? Five hundred years old? A thousand years old? Some say he comes all the way from the Fall. Some say that he existed before the Fall. If I tell you more about him it will become a little clearer just who he is.

He is very impolite. He has never read any rules of etiquette or polite behaviour, or, if he has read them, he certainly does not apply them. He always enters your home uninvited and the minute he arrives he takes the floor and begins to accuse you. You may not like it but he continues to accuse you, and he stays as long as he likes.

Of course, it is by now evident that this mysterious visitor is none other than conscience. In a book by John Mackenzie, a renowned psychologist, we are told that mental health institutions are filled with people suffering from a repressed or guilty conscience. And I remember how Dr Mulder, a very close friend of mine who was the superintendent of a psychiatric hospital in the United States, used to tell me the same thing, that many people were in his hospital suffering from a guilty conscience.

The conscience is a very great problem for people, because we all want to be 'accepted'. Not so long ago the newspapers carried an item about a young man who was not accepted by his college fraternity, and he committed suicide on that account. But the most tragic thing of all is not to be accepted by God.

The Dutch have a few poetic lines which say that at the root of every problem is the matter of man's guilt, and so it is. Now this is the problem laid before us in the *Epistle to the Romans*. To be sure it is a theme which runs right through the Bible, with Job, for example, asking, 'How can a man be right with God?' That is what *Romans* is all about.

This evening, I will give you just a 'look' at *Romans*, and, in the last few minutes, a look at the author of *Romans*. This epistle, as you perhaps know already, consists of two main parts. The doctrinal part comprises the first eleven chapters (justification by faith), and then from chapter 12 to 16 we read about the duties of those who have been justified by faith; the duties of their relationship to God, to their fellow-believers, to the ruling power, and also to everyone else.

Sad and sombre, dark and dismal, is the picture Paul draws of the heathen world in the first chapter of *Romans*. When you read that chapter you are struck especially by the fact that so many of the sins mentioned there are also very prevalent today.

Then in the second chapter (and up to the eighth verse of the third chapter), Paul sizes up the world of the Jews, asking, 'You Jew, are you any better?' 'No,' he replies, 'you are no better.'

Then, when he reaches the ninth verse of the third chapter he addresses himself very definitely to the congregation at Rome, and says, 'Are we any better? I have laid bare the sinfulness of the heathen world and also of the Jewish world, and now I must be very personal – What about you and me?' His conclusion is that we are no better by nature, because the whole world is in a state of guilt before God. Then he builds on that fact for a while, and declares that –

'There is none righteous, no, not one: there is none that understandeth, there is none that seeketh after God. They are all gone out of the way, they are together become unprofitable; there is none that doeth good, no, not one.

'Their throat is an open sepulchre; with their tongues they have used deceit; the poison of asps is under their lips: whose mouth is full of cursing and bitterness: their feet are swift to shed blood: destruction and misery are in their ways: and the way of peace have they not known: there is no fear of God before their eyes.'

This is a terrible description of a terrible situation. The question arises, what now? In these first three chapters of *Romans* we have pointed out to us the pressing need, and the reality of justification by faith. Having thus pictured the situation in the world of the Jews and of the Gentiles, Paul's great question is – How can the soul be accepted with God?

The idea of many Jews, especially the scholars among them, was that by trying their utmost to obey all the commandments one might perhaps be able to become right with God. There were even some rabbis who claimed that they had actually succeeded in keeping all the commandments of God. By this they meant not only the written law, but even the oral law which they said had also been conveyed by God to Moses at Sinai, and had also been passed down the generations, a law for just about every situation in life. But the more realistic people, those who had a truer assessment of themselves, realised that perfect righteousness was just impossible. Here is a picture in verse of a person striving for acceptance with God by his own personal righteousness, and then discovering justification by faith alone:–

> O long and dark the stairs I trod
> With trembling feet to find my God,
> Gaining a foothold bit by bit,
> Then slipping back and losing it.
>
> Never progressing; striving still,
> With weakening grasp and faltering will,
> Bleeding to climb to God, while He
> Serenely smiled, not noting me.
>
> Then came a certain time when I
> Loosened my hold and fell thereby;
> Down to the lowest step my fall,
> As if I had not climbed at all.
>
> Now when I lay despairing there,
> Listen . . . a footfall on the stair,
> On that same stair where I, afraid,
> Faltered and fell and lay dismayed.
> And lo, when hope had ceased to be,
> My God came down the stairs to me.

'Justified freely by his grace through the redemption that is in Christ Jesus' *(Romans 3.24!)* – that is the text in these verses is it not? The poem shows plainly the atmosphere of the text.

In the fourth chapter of *Romans*, Paul shows that this concept of justification by grace through faith is not a novelty. People might well say, 'Paul, this is something new that you present to us. Our rabbis have never told us this, and we trust our rabbis. They all say that we must earn our way into Heaven, and now you come up with this.'

So Paul shows that this teaching of justification by faith, purely by the grace of God, is not a novelty at all. Already in the first chapter he has hinted that there is a text in *Habakkuk 2.4* that one must not forget – 'The just shall live by his faith.'

But now, when he speaks about this in more detail, he naturally refers to *Genesis 15.6*, where Abraham believed God and it was reckoned to him for righteousness, without his earning it. So Paul shows that the redemption in Christ, which was coming down the line of the ages, was already reckoned to Abraham for righteousness.

Then Paul also quotes from *Psalm 32*, where David says, 'Blessed is he whose transgression is forgiven, whose sin is covered. Blessed is the man unto whom the Lord imputeth *[reckons]* not iniquity.'

In chapters 5, 6, 7 and 8 of *Romans* the doctrine of justification by faith is presented as being effective. It is needed and it is real, as we are told in the first three chapters. It is scriptural and based upon the Old Testament as we are told in the fourth chapter. And now, in these chapters, we are shown that it is actually effective to save, producing rich fruit.

There is a logical way of remembering the principles taught in chapters 5 to 8 – a little memory bridge. Remember that Paul teaches here the philosophy of redemption. The first four consonants in the word philosophy – p, h, l and s – provide the memory bridge.

In the fifth chapter the fruit which is emphasised is peace. 'Being justified by faith, we have peace with God through our Lord Jesus Christ.' The sixth chapter has as its key word – holiness.

The seventh chapter deals with liberty, that is, freedom from the law in a spiritual sense. And then the beautiful eighth chapter emphasises super-invincibility. Invincibility means that a man cannot be conquered, but to be super-invincible means that he is more than a conqueror. All things work together for good to them that love God, even trials and enemies.

But let us go back to that fifth chapter for a moment, the theme of being justified by faith. What is meant by being justified? There is, of course, a theological definition which we may give very learnedly. We can say that justification is that act of God the Father whereby He pronounces the sinner just, on the basis of the vicarious atonement of Christ. But we need something more stirring than even that fine definition.

We may imagine the case of an orphan who grew up to be a young man and then fell to a powerful temptation. Imagine he was in the position where he had access to government secrets and was offered a huge sum of money by a foreign government to communicate those secrets to them. He committed treason and was discovered and exposed.

The law of the land said that those guilty of treason must suffer the death penalty, and eventually the young man found himself in a courtroom with no effective defence. He was duly found guilty, and before passing sentence the judge finally and formally asked if he had anything to say. At this point, when all seemed lost, a letter arrived in the courtroom, and the judge opened it. It was a pardon, issued by the only person in that country who was authorised to write such a pardon – the king.

Justification is just such a pardon, for we have all betrayed ourselves to Satan and served him in so many ways. But justification is such a beautiful doctrine that we must take our simple illustration a little further.

The young man went out of the courtroom and was naturally congratulated by many friends and so on. But the next day, a truly astonishing occurrence took place, for the king visited his house, and the king said to him, 'We have longed for many years to have a son, and you are an orphan. We would like to adopt you as our son.' So he was adopted into the family of the king.

Beloved friends in the Lord Jesus Christ, that is what has happened to us. Not only have we been pardoned on the basis of no good-ness or deserving in ourselves, but also we have been adopted as the sons and daughters of the King of kings. In human affairs, adoption always brings great uncertainty. We all know of people who have adopted a child and everything went very well. The child grew up to be well-behaved and a real joy to the adopting parents. But we doubtless all know of other cases where the people who adopted a child would have liked so much to have conveyed their spirit to the child, but it never happened. The child became a problem child.

The beauty of justification, with its pardon and adoption, is brought out in *Romans 8.15* (and many other verses in *Romans*). Not only does God pardon and adopt us on the basis of the merits of our Lord and Saviour Jesus Christ, but also He imparts to us His own Spirit, the Spirit of adoption, so that we receive His standards and love His lordship over us, and are able to cry out with all our hearts – 'Abba, Father!' Is this not a wonderful doctrine? This is justification.

Romans 5 sings its way along and mentions many other blessings in connection with the peace that results from justification. We have assurance of salvation, and a peace which the little boy in Sunday School once defined as 'God smiling in my heart'.

What illustration shall we use to do justice to the peace of God which settles in our hearts when we are justified? Shall we think of the peace of the cemetery, where nothing stirs? Of course not. That is the peace of dead bones. Shall we think perhaps of the peace of a bright afternoon, the air invigorating and exhilarating, the cattle grazing on the pasture lands, the farmer on his porch reading, altogether a beautiful scene of rural peace? This is alright, but it is not good enough to illustrate spiritual peace.

Shall we think, perhaps, of the peace of the evening, the blue of the evening sky full of silent beauty and majesty with its myriads of scintillating lights, sparkling like so many dew drops on the diamonds of the heavens? This is wonderful, and it causes us to cry out, 'Oh God – Thou art my God!' And yet I would say that even this is not the illustration we are looking for.

Rather, my dear friends in the Lord, if we want to receive an adequate impression of the peace which Paul speaks of, then we must think along these lines:– The lightning flashes and the thunder roars, and all the black-coated legions of the storm stand overhead. It is a dreadful scene. But in the cleft of the rock there is a little bird, perhaps your nightingale, or perhaps our mockingbird. The little bird is sheltered completely from the storm, warbling its sweet and melodious song in perfect peace. Is not this the picture?

The thunder and the lightning descended at Calvary on to the head and the heart of our Saviour, Jesus Christ, and we are sheltered by Him, and what He has done on our behalf. That is why we can sing so joyfully of an experience of peace in our hearts.

In the sixth chapter of *Romans*, the theme is holiness or holy living. 'What shall we say then? Shall we continue in sin, that grace may abound?' We learn from this that there were actually people who said that a man did not have to attempt to be holy at all because it would all come by grace. And so in order to give grace an opportunity to operate, they could indulge in sin and 'live it up', for the more sin there was in the life, the more grace would have a chance to operate.

This was terrible wickedness, but it was an attitude which seems to have been quite prevalent in the early church. Paul refers to it in *Romans 3.8* as well as in this sixth chapter. Also, in *2 Peter 3.16* we see that Peter speaks of the apostle Paul's writings, and adds the words – 'which they that are unlearned and unstable wrest, as they do also the other scriptures, unto their own destruction.' Very likely he was talking about the same distortion – the notion that we may sin so that grace may abound.

If we read the *Epistle of Jude*, we find Jude saying, 'I was about to write an epistle to you on the subject of our common salvation, when I was suddenly compelled to write about something else, namely about these men who change the grace of God into lasciviousness.'

The doctrine of grace cannot be turned into an excuse for immoral living, so Paul emphasises that the wages of sin is death, but the free gift of God is everlasting life through Jesus Christ our Lord. Throughout chapter 6 he emphasises that holiness (or sanctified living) is an essential consequence of true justification.

The theme of the much-discussed seventh chapter of *Romans* is liberty. But in what sense are we free from the law? Certainly not in every sense. We are set free in the sense that we are no longer under the curse of the law. But we are also freed in the sense that the law is not for us the means of becoming saved (and what a hopeless, unattainable means of salvation it would be).

In the first part of *Romans 7* (the first thirteen verses) Paul seems to be speaking as a typical believer about his own life before grace entered. He constantly uses the past tense. Then, when we come to the fourteenth verse (running to the end of the chapter) the debate begins. What does Paul mean in these verses? He uses expressions such as, 'I am carnal, sold under sin . . . The good that I would I do not: but the evil which I would not, that I do . . . Wretched man that I am! who shall deliver me from the body of this death? I thank God through Jesus Christ our Lord.' There has probably been more literature published on this section than on any other section in *Romans*.

It is my conviction, having read all the arguments on both sides, that Paul is speaking in these verses of himself as a Christian believer (and also of all other similar believers). My reasons are as follows. First of all, the change in the tense is significant. Paul has been describing himself as he was in the past, and now, beginning at the fourteenth verse, he constantly uses the present tense as if to tell us that his situation is now as he is describing it.

The second reason why I believe Paul is speaking about himself as a believer is that I cannot understand how an unbeliever would be able to say that he delighted in the law of God after the inner man. But this is what Paul says here. Nor do I believe that an unbeliever would ever be able to say, 'O wretched man that I am! who shall deliver me from the body of this death? I thank God through Jesus Christ our Lord.' If this is not the language of a Christian, I do not know what it is.

There is one more argument, and it is this. Friends who take the opposite view usually point out that Paul uses extreme expressions, describing a 'wretched man', and a man who is unable to do the good he wants to do, or to resist the evil which he does not want to do. The man in this passage is described as 'carnal'. How could a Christian ever say such things about himself?

Personally, I do not find any difficulty with these expressions, for I believe, on the basis of what I have heard from people after being in the ministry a good many years, and on the basis of what I read in Scripture, that the further people advance along the pathway of sanctification, the more humbly they will express themselves concerning their spiritual condition. Remember how Paul tells us in *1 Corinthians 15* that he is not worthy to be called an apostle. It is also Paul who tells us in *Ephesians 3* that he is less than the least of all the saints. Again, Paul tells us in *1 Timothy 1* that he is the chief of sinners.

Is it therefore so strange that he should say what he says at the end of the seventh chapter of *Romans*? And it is not only Paul who speaks this way about his own sinfulness. Think of other holy men of God pictured to us in Scripture. Think of Job who at the end of the story says, 'Wherefore I abhor myself, and repent in dust and ashes.' This is strong language. Or think of Isaiah, that godly man, that majestic prophet, saying, 'I am a man of unclean lips.' Such men were able to say these things because they knew their hearts, they knew their sinfulness, even though they were true believers.

Romans 8 brings us to the concept of super-invincibility, or of being 'more than conquerors'. In this chapter Paul summons, as it were, all the possible enemies who would seek to lay him low and oppose him. He summons all the forces that would rob him of his faith or joy. He considers suffering (verse 18) and concludes that 'the sufferings of this present time are not worthy to be compared with the glory which shall be revealed in us.'

He considers Satan and his accusations and concludes that 'if God be for us, who can be against us?' As he takes all these difficulties and enemies in turn, he tells us that, rightly considered, all things, even these difficulties and enemies, work together for good to those who love God and who are the called according to His purpose.

'What shall we then say to these things? If God be for us, who can be against us? He that spared not his own Son, but delivered him up for us all, how shall he not with him also freely give us all things?

'Who shall lay any thing to the charge of God's elect? It is God that justifieth. Who is he that condemneth? It is Christ that died, yea rather, that is risen again, who is even at the right hand of God, who also maketh intercession for us.

'Who shall separate us from the love of Christ? shall tribulation, or distress, or persecution, or famine, or nakedness, or peril, or sword? As it is written, For thy sake we are killed all the day long; we are accounted as sheep for the slaughter.

'Nay, in all these things we are more than conquerors through him that loved us. For I am persuaded, that neither death, nor life, nor angels, nor principalities, nor powers, nor things present, nor things to come, nor height, nor depth, nor any other creature, shall be able to separate us from the love of God, which is in Christ Jesus our Lord.' Here is the wonderful spiritual super-invincibility of a child of God, safe in Jesus Christ.

Finally, let us look briefly at the author of *Romans*. Paul was a man with an iron will, a very keen intellect and a warm, loving heart. What this man was not willing to sacrifice for Christ! Before he wrote *Romans* he wrote *1* and *2 Corinthians*. Just think of the sufferings he was willing to endure for the Lord Jesus Christ, as recorded in *2 Corinthians 11.24-28:*

'Of the Jews five times received I forty stripes save one. Thrice was I beaten with rods, once was I stoned, thrice I suffered shipwreck, a night and a day I have been in the deep; in journeyings often, in perils of waters, in perils of robbers, in perils by mine own countrymen, in perils by the heathen, in perils in the city, in perils in the wilderness, in perils in the sea, in perils among false brethren; in weariness and painfulness, in watchings often, in hunger and thirst, in fastings often, in cold and nakedness. Beside those things that are without, that which cometh upon me daily, the care of all the churches.'

What was the special personal emphasis of this wonderful man? To find out, read *1 Corinthians 9.22* and then also verse 27:

'To the weak became I as weak, that I might gain the weak: I am made all things to all men, that I might by all means save some.'

'But I keep under my body, and bring it into subjection: lest that by any means, when I have preached to others, I myself should be a castaway.'

I am so deeply in sympathy with all work which emphasises evangelisation, mission activity and outreach, for this is exactly what Paul emphasised. We should stress this also. But then we must remember how he was prepared to beat or 'pommel' his body lest 'having preached to others, I myself would be rejected'. In other words, when you or I go out and ring doorbells, or in any other way try to bring people to Christ, we had better do it tremblingly. We had better go privately to the Lord first of all and say, 'Oh Lord, be Thou merciful to me a sinner.' How good are we; how bad? How far do we fall short? Holiness is a central part of our programme and we must never forget it.

Perhaps someone asks the inward question – If I compare myself with a man like Paul, who am I? I am not in such a position of opportunity, or in possession of such gifts. What can I do for the Lord? The answer is to remember always the thoroughly biblical, Pauline theme captured in the following lines:–

> *If you cannot on the ocean*
> *Sail among the swiftest fleet,*
> *Rocking o'er the highest billows,*
> *Laughing at the storms you meet;*
> *You can stand among the sailors*
> *Anchored still, within the bay,*
> *You can lend a hand to help them*
> *As they launch their boats away.*
>
> *If you are too weak to journey*
> *Up the mountains steep and high,*
> *You can stand within the valley*
> *While the multitudes go by;*
> *You can chant in happy measure*

As they slowly pass along,
Though they may forget the singer
They will not forget the song.

If you have not gold or silver
Ever ready at command,
If you cannot toward the needy
Stretch an ever-open hand;
You can comfort the afflicted,
O'er the erring you can weep;
You can be Christ's true disciple –
Sitting at the Master's feet.

If you cannot, in the battle,
Prove yourself a soldier true;
If, where fire and smoke are thickest,
There's no work for you to do;
When the battlefield is silent,
You can go with careful tread,
You can bear away the wounded,
You can cover up the dead.

Do not then stand idly waiting
For some greater work to do;
Fortune is a lazy goddess,
She will never come to you;
Go and work in any vineyard;
Do not fail to do and dare;
If you want a field of labour
You will find it – anywhere!

Ellen M. H. Gates
1835-1920

2

Trust, Try, Travel and Triumph
A Survey of Philippians

WHEN PAUL WROTE his letter to the Romans, he stated his plan of travel and told them that his prayer was to visit them on his way to Spain. He said, 'First of all, I have to deliver a gift for the poor saints in Jerusalem, so I will be travelling there. And from there I will be going to Spain and I will stop in Rome and see you all before travelling on, if God wills, of course.'

As you probably know, God willed differently. What actually happened is that Paul went to Jerusalem, was captured there, and spent a couple of years' imprisonment in Caesarea. Then, later on, he appealed to Caesar and finally arrived in Rome as a prisoner.

He lived for a while, as Luke tells us, as a prisoner in a rented house, and while in Rome he wrote several letters. He wrote a letter to the Colossians, and one to Philemon. He wrote a letter to the Ephesians, and, very likely last of all during that imprisonment, he wrote his letter to the Philippians. Whether at the time he was still living in his rented home is quite a question. Most interpreters believe that by the time of the Philippian letter he was suffering a more rigorous imprisonment.

The reason why Paul was writing to the Philippians at that time is that he had received an abundant gift from this very generous church. It had been delivered to him by Epaphroditus, one of the spiritual leaders of the church at Philippi, and so this is really a 'thank you' letter. At the same time it is also a message of reassurance, because Epaphroditus had become very ill and had nearly died, so Paul wrote to assure the Philippians that he was well again and would soon see them.

As to the content of the letter, it seems to me that once you know it you can never forget it. You can, of course, organise this letter to the Philippians chapter-by-chapter, as I have done in my commentary, but you can also organise the material in an entirely different way, which I am going to do here. I am going to suggest four verbs for its division of themes, all beginning with the same letter, for convenience. The first (which is the key word of *Philippians* chapter 1) would be *trust*.

There were possibly three reasons why the Philippians needed an exhortation to trust. They seemed to have become anxious and worried. *Philippians* is one letter in which Paul says, 'Be not anxious' (in chapter 4). If they were not actually worried at the time Paul wrote, there was a danger that they might become very worried about three matters. First, they were liable to be anxious about themselves. They had become believers, but would they remain that way? Was there not every possibility that they would lose their faith and not be saved in the end?

Secondly, they were liable to be anxious about the Gospel, because Paul was in prison in Rome, suffering sometimes a milder, sometimes a harsher level of severity, so what would become of the Gospel there? Thirdly, they were liable to worry about yet another problem, and that concerned Paul himself. His sentence of acquittal or condemnation was about to be given; which would it be? Were they going to lose Paul? Would he be condemned to death?

These were the three worries, as we can see by reading the epistle, and we have Paul's answer to these concerns in chapter 1 verses 6, 12, 20 and 21. In verse 6 he answers their possible worry about the permanence of their salvation, effectively saying, 'I am convinced that He Who began a good work in you will surely not let you down, but will continue that good work all the way with His Church until Christ comes again.'

This is what we often call the doctrine of the perseverance of the saints, a doctrine taught all through the Bible. We find it, for example, in *Psalm 89.33* where we read about God's faithfulness which will never be removed. *John 3.16* tells us about a life which will never end. *John 4.14* speaks about a well of water which, once it has entered the soul of a person, will continue to spring up unto everlasting life. In *John 10.28* we hear the Saviour say, 'And I give unto them eternal life; and they shall never perish, neither shall any man pluck them out of my hand.' Of course, we see it so clearly in *Romans 8* – where we read of a love from which we can never be separated. Then *Romans 11.29* assures us that the calling of God can never be revoked.

2 Timothy 2.19 gives us the illustration of the foundation which cannot be shaken, and *1 Peter 1.4* holds before us the picture of an inheritance which is reserved and which can never fade away. What a firm foundation for our faith we have! Is it not wonderful? Calvinism is surely in accordance with the Bible.

The second worry of the Philippians was that Paul's imprisonment would put the Gospel at risk. In *Philippians 1.12* Paul assures them: 'You do not need to be worried about the Gospel. The things which have happened to me have fallen out rather to the advantage of the Gospel. You do not need to be anxious about that.

'Events have worked to the advantage of the Gospel in two ways,' says Paul. 'First, because it is being noised abroad in the entire praetorian guard that my bonds are for Christ. Why, these soldiers, who guard me by rotation, are talking it over with each other. They tell each other that I am not a criminal, but that I am here for the sake of Christ. In this way they begin to enquire and talk about Christ. Some of them have become Christians and they talk to all the others in the garrison, even those of Caesar's household.'

Paul's imprisonment, therefore, is leading to the spread of the Gospel in a very crucial place. Also, Paul tells them, the Gospel is prospering because the Christians in the area of Rome, that is to say the leaders or ministers, are becoming far more bold because of his own example. Through seeing the manner in which he endures his imprisonment, others are becoming far more bold to proclaim the good tidings.

Sadly, not all of them do it with proper motivation; while some of them preach the Gospel from the motivation of love for God, for the Gospel and for Paul, others are moved by considerations which are not so pure, wanting to raise up hardship for Paul in his bonds. Imagine that! Is it not terrible that there are ministers of the Gospel who preach the Gospel from impure motives because they are moved by jealousy? Perhaps the minister in the next church has a bigger crowd, and so they are jealous, and they begin to work against him. It should not be, but throughout all the ages these things have been, and are.

But Paul is a big man, spiritually speaking. It is very likely that he was a small man physically, but spiritually he is a big man with a big soul, and so he says, 'After all, the great thing is that Christ is being proclaimed, and in that I rejoice, and I will rejoice.'

The other worry of the Philippians centred on the well-being of the apostle. What would happen to him? He deals with this anxiety in verses 20 and 21 of this first chapter. They do not need to worry about him. What matters, he tells them, is solely that – 'Christ shall be magnified in my body, whether it be by life, or by death. For to me to live is Christ, and to die is gain.'

'Oh,' he says, 'I know I am often caught in between two desires and pressed from both sides. To be with Christ would be far better for me personally, but on the other hand I also realise you need me, and so for your sake I would hope to stay. I feel that I will stay, to be of benefit to you all.'

Now that is a little summary, or 'a look' at the first chapter. The emphasis has been on trust. Do not be so worried. Trust God – all things will be well.

> *Oh for a faith that will not shrink,*
> *Though pressed by every foe;*
> *That will not tremble on the brink*
> *Of any earthly woe.*

Says the apostle, 'Oh, give us such a faith as this, so that whatever may come, we will taste even here the blessedness of the eternal home. Give us such a faith!'

As we now move to the second chapter, the key word is one that follows naturally after trust. The key word of this second chapter is *try*, or you might also say *work*. (In order to secure a word which begins with the same letter so that it is easier to remember the plan of the epistle, we prefer *try*.) This truly is the keynote of the second chapter as we see plainly on reading verses 12 and 13:–

'Work out your own salvation with fear and trembling. For it is God which worketh in you both to will and to do of his good pleasure.'

Paul is very careful not to co-ordinate our work and God's work as if the one is just as important as the other. He carefully states the relationship between the two. We work not in our own power, but rather because we know that God is doing His work in us, we work by His power; but we must work. This work idea is emphasised through the entire chapter. First of all we have a few verses in which we find emphasis upon harmony, humility and helpfulness, the three 'h's of verses 2, 3 and 4, where these duties are set out. Says Paul:–

'Fulfil ye my joy, that ye be likeminded, having the same love, being of one accord, of one mind. Let nothing be done through strife or vainglory; but in lowliness of mind let each esteem other better than themselves. Look not every man on his own things, but every man also on the things of others.'

Then, beginning with the fifth verse, Paul continues the theme of work by showing what Christ has done. The Saviour did not sit still when He saw our plight and misery from Heaven. Though He was rich, He became poor that we through His poverty might become rich. That is the essence of what Paul says here. 'Have this mind in you,' says the apostle, 'which was also in Christ Jesus, Who, existing in the essence of God (the form of God), was willing to empty Himself.'

Of what did He empty Himself? Some people think He emptied Himself of His deity, but that is certainly wrong. Though existing in the form of God, He emptied Himself –

'. . . and took upon him the form of a servant, and was made in the likeness of men: and being found in fashion as a man, he humbled himself, and became obedient unto death, even the death of the cross. Wherefore God also hath highly exalted him, and given him a name which is above every name: that at the name of Jesus every knee should bow, of things in heaven, and things in earth, and things under the earth; and that every tongue should confess that Jesus Christ is Lord, to the glory of God the Father.'

In other words, Jesus did something – He worked. The emphasis in this second chapter is not so much upon doctrine as upon ethics. Because the section starts with the words – 'Have this mind in you which was also in Christ Jesus' – we know we are to do something. He worked, or did something, to help us. So also we should work, as verse 12 tells us. In other words, Jesus worked for us, and He worked on such a vast scale that we cannot begin to work as He did, but certainly we should work in response.

Toward the end of the chapter (from verse 19) we notice that Paul himself was also a constant worker or trier. He might well have put a sign on his prison door reading, 'Mission Headquarters', because from his prison he carried out so much evangelistic work.

In the last part of the chapter he tells us what he is going to do, naming the person he will send to each place. He says, 'I am going to send Timothy to you.' And then he describes Timothy, saying, 'I can depend on him, because he works just like a son will work for his father. I cannot depend on the others so well. They are thinking of their own business. But Timothy, he is engrossed entirely in the Gospel.' Then he adds a little note, saying that he hopes to visit them himself before long, and his hope was granted, because he actually was released from that imprisonment.

Remember the central verse of this second chapter. Since Jesus Christ did all that work for you, and since I am doing so much work from my prison, 'work out your own salvation with fear and trembling.' 'Work,' says the apostle. 'Strive! Do something!'

> Did you ever plant a garden
>   With a love to see things grow?
> Then you know that every morning
>   It means hoe! hoe! hoe!
>
> Were you ever in a vineyard
>   When the grapes were ripe and thick?
> When you came to fill your basket,
>   It meant pick! pick! pick!
>
> Did you ever learn a lesson
>   Just by lying down to cry?
> Or was this your resolution,
>   I will try, try, try?

To be always trying does not mean that we always have to see a successful end. Some people seem to think that way. Unless they are sure that their spiritual work is going to result in immediate success they will not engage in it. But that is so foolish, as we learn from Solomon – 'Cast thy bread upon the waters: for thou shalt find it after many days' (Ecclesiastes 11.1). Seemingly unrewarded toil gives unexpected long-term results, as an old comic poem points out:–

> Two frogs fell into a deep cream bowl,
> The one was an optimistic soul.
> But the other took a different view,
> 'We shall drown,' he said, without further ado.
>
> So, with a last despairing cry,
> He threw up his legs, and went on to die.
> But the other said, with a merry grin,
> 'Though I can't jump out, I'll not give in.
>
> 'I'll just swim, and swim, till my strength is spent,
> And then if I die, well, I'll die more content!'
> So he swam and he swam, till it would seem,
> As if the swimming had churned the cream.
>
> So at last, on top of the butter he stopped,
> And gaily out of the pot he hopped.
> The moral here is easily found,
> If you can't jump out, just keep swimming around.

In chapter 1 we saw that the theme was *trust*. In the second chapter it was *try*. Now, in the third chapter, we find that the theme is *travel*, not travelling along, but travelling upward, excelsior! *Travel* is the key word of the chapter. In the first part of the third chapter, Paul is warning against Judaizers, and in the last part he is warning against paganizers. In between, he tells believers to follow his own example of travelling upward, striving to become more holy and fit for the Master's use all the time. That is the chief idea of the third chapter.

'Finally, my brethren,' he starts out, 'rejoice in the Lord. To write the same things to you, to me indeed is not grievous, but for you it is safe.' Then he warns them, 'Beware of dogs, beware of evil workers, beware of the concision. For we are the circumcision, which worship God in the spirit, and rejoice in Christ Jesus, and have no confidence in the flesh.' After the warning about placing confidence in the flesh, he begins to swing upwards, or to travel up, as we see in the eighth verse:

'Yea doubtless, and I count all things but loss for the excellency of the knowledge of Christ Jesus my Lord: for whom I have suffered the loss of all things, and do count them but dung, that I may win Christ . . . that I may know him, and the power of his resurrection.'

'I do not claim that I am already perfect,' he says, 'but one thing I do: forgetting what lies behind, and straining forward to that which lies ahead, I press on for the goal with a view to the upward call of God in Christ Jesus.' That should be our ideal also.

As we come to the end of the third chapter we find Paul levelling charges against the paganizers. He says that his readers should imitate him, and should mark those others who lived and walked as he did. There were so many, said Paul, who walked differently. 'I told you that when I was among you, and I say now, with weeping, that they are enemies of the Cross of Christ. Their end is perdition. Their god is their belly. Their glory is their shame. They seek earthly things.'

'Our expectation (by contrast) is from Heaven. That is our commonwealth. We are a colony of Heaven. Our homeland is in Heaven, from where we expect the Saviour, Jesus Christ, Who will refashion the body of our humiliation so that it will be conformed to the body of His glory. And He will do it by that power which allows Him and enables Him to subject all things to Himself.'

So far we have observed that the chapters have the key themes of trust, try, and *travel*. In other words, we should never be satisfied. Always we should strive to do more and better things for the Lord, and to not say 'no' when we are called upon. As we come to the last chapter, the key word is undoubtedly *triumph*, for this chapter is about triumph in trial. After reading the eleventh and thirteenth verses there can be no doubt that this is the key word: 'For I have learned, in whatsoever state I am, therewith to be content . . . I can do all things through Christ which strengtheneth me.' When a person is able to say these words, then he is, in a sense, having Heaven on earth. He is living the triumphant life even here. He is feasting on the joys and the triumphs of Heaven.

At the beginning of the chapter Paul shows how much he thinks of the church at Philippi: 'Therefore, my brethren dearly beloved and longed for, my joy and crown, so stand fast in the Lord, my dearly beloved.' Paul never wrote to any other church in such a manner. Philippi was a church of workers, of encouragers, of people who were always helping out the cause. There are usually a number of such people in every congregation, but in some congregations there are only a few. Everyone, of course, should be like those people.

This was the church of Lydia who said to Paul, Silas, Timothy and Dr Luke, the missionaries who arrived in Philippi, 'Come into my house and stay here.' She did not mind at all. She must have been a woman of some wealth, and she had a spacious house, but she was so devoted to Christ after her conversion that she was willing to yield everything to Him and for Him. 'Come, missionaries,' she said, 'make my house your headquarters.' And that spirit of Lydia must have been very contagious, for wherever Paul went there was always a gift from the church at Philippi.

Then, after the wonderful introduction to chapter 4, Paul gives two ladies a telling off, saying, 'I beseech Euodias, and beseech Syntyche, that they be of the same mind in the Lord.' Imagine the scene if these ladies were in the church when the letter was read out to everyone! But notice what else Paul does. He not only reprimands them, but at the same time he praises them, for he says, 'I exhort you Syzygus . . .' This is a Greek name which means yokefellow, and no doubt he was a real, genuine Syzygus! He must have been a leader in the congregation. 'You are true to your name,' says Paul, 'you are a true yokefellow, and I exhort you to help these women for they struggled along with me, side by side with me, in the Gospel.' Now he praises them. He publicly remembers what wonderful women they were when they struggled to help him for the sake of the Gospel. If ever we have someone to reprimand, if possible we find out something about the good which that person does, and then our admonition is far more effective. Let Paul be our example.

As Paul continues to remember his other 'fellowlabourers' he mentions that their names are in the Book of Life, and when he mentions that Book of Life, then he immediately exclaims –

'Rejoice in the Lord alway: and again I say, Rejoice. Let your moderation be known unto all men. The Lord is at hand. Be careful for nothing; but in every thing by prayer and supplication with thanksgiving let your requests be made known unto God. And the peace of God, which passeth all understanding, shall keep your hearts and minds through Christ Jesus.'

At the very beginning of the epistle Paul began with prayer, telling the Philippians how often he prayed for them. Now, at the close, he again exhorts them to pray. In other words, all our trusting, all our trying, and all our travelling will mean nothing unless we depend entirely upon God and seek Him often in prayer.

Then, finally, Paul gives us the secret of how to endure trials and come out triumphant in all our thinking and actions. Here is a summary of Christian duty – a list of our proper motives, manners and morals. Here is the right pasture for Christians to graze in. All Christian duty may be expressed in this one thought – that in all their thinking (with a view to future deeds) believers should strive to overcome evil with good. Those things which are true, honourable, just, pure, lovely, and of good report must crowd out all that is base. The reward of the peace of God will be ours, and the God of peace will be with us.

'Finally, brethren, whatsoever things are true, whatsoever things are honest, whatsoever things are just, whatsoever things are pure, whatsoever things are lovely, whatsoever things are of good report; if there be any virtue, and if there be any praise, think on these things. Those things, which ye have both learned, and received, and heard, and seen in me, do: and the God of peace shall be with you.'

In other words, God has given us whatever we need to know in this beautiful epistle, to *trust, try, travel* upwards, and so to *triumph* in the Lord.

3
Four Special Features
of Luke's Gospel

S O THAT WE can appreciate what is so very precious about the *Gospel of Luke*, we may view it in four ways. It is first of all a book of *doctrine*. Secondly, it is a book of *ethics*, telling us how to live. Thirdly, it is a book of *comfort*, which explains to us why we should rejoice. And finally, it is a book of *prophecy*, telling us what to expect. In this very short look at *Luke*, I will give just an example or two of each emphasis, though of course, there are very many more examples that could be given.

1. A Book of Doctrine

As we consider the very beginning of *Luke's Gospel* we realise that it is a book of doctrine, for we read:

'Forasmuch as many have taken in hand to set forth in order a declaration of those things which are most surely believed among us, even as they delivered them unto us, which from the beginning were eyewitnesses, and ministers of the word; it seemed good to me also, having had perfect understanding of all things from the very first, to write unto thee in order, most excellent Theophilus, that thou mightest know the certainty of those things, wherein thou hast been instructed.'

Luke's Gospel, for example, places great emphasis on the doctrine of predestination. We glory in that doctrine and we love our God all the more for it, for we realise that it is the very foundation of our salvation.

> 'Tis not that I did choose Thee,
> For, Lord, that could not be,
> This heart would still refuse Thee,
> But Thou hast chosen me.

This is the tenor of *Luke's Gospel*. Of course, it is also true of the other Gospels and of the whole Word of God, but it is very emphatically true of *Luke*. There is a note of election sounded in the song of the angels recorded in *Luke 2.14*: 'Glory to God in the highest, and on earth peace, to men of His good pleasure' – indicating that these were God's pleasure from all eternity. Luke and Paul were intimate friends, as you know, and Paul speaks very much about this doctrine of predestination, especially in *Ephesians 1.3*: 'Blessed be the God and Father of our Lord Jesus Christ, who hath blessed us with all spiritual blessings in heavenly places in Christ: according as he hath chosen us in him before the foundation of the world, that we should be holy and without blame before him.' And then, in *Ephesians 1.5*, he says – 'according to the good pleasure of his will'.

This is exactly Luke's terminology in the song of the angels, and we find it repeatedly in *Luke's Gospel*, where it is clear that the solid foundation of our salvation is that it rests on the will and good pleasure of God.

Luke 10.20 deals with the return of the seventy missionaries who rejoice because even the demons have been subject to them. Then

Jesus says, 'Rejoice not, that the spirits are subject unto you; but rather rejoice, because your names are written in heaven.' There again is the thought of predestination. And when we go on to *Luke 12.32*, we read – 'Fear not, little flock; for it is your Father's good pleasure to give you the kingdom.' Another example occurs in *Luke 18.7* in the words – 'Shall not God avenge his own elect, which cry day and night unto him?'

This doctrine of election occurs yet again in *Luke 22.22* – 'The Son of man goeth, as it was determined: but woe unto that man by whom he is betrayed!' This last passage is also found in *Matthew 26* and *Mark 14*, but it is clear that there is a particular emphasis on predestination in *Luke*, and this continues in *Acts*. In *Acts 2.23*, for example, Luke says – 'Him, being delivered by the determinate counsel and foreknowledge of God, ye have taken, and by wicked hands have crucified and slain.' Once again, in *Acts 13.48*, we find predestination in the words – 'And as many as were ordained to eternal life believed.' So we could go on quoting verses from these two books from Luke. An old hymn truly reflects this emphasis of Luke:–

I sing the gracious, fixed decree,
Passed by the great Eternal Three:
The counsel, wrought in Heaven above,
The Lord's predestinating love.

All that concerns the chosen race,
(And nature, history embrace)
Where they shall live, and when remove –
Fixed by predestinating love.

Their calling, growth, and robes they wear,
Their conflicts, trials, daily care,
Are for them well arranged above,
In God's predestinating love.

In this let Zion's sons rejoice,
Their God will not revoke His choice;
Not sin, or death or hell can move,
His firm predestinating love.

This is our bulwark of defence:
Nor friend nor foe shall drive us hence;
In life and death, in realms above,
We'll sing predestinating love!

This is but one strand by way of example of the emphasis which Luke gives to doctrinal matters in his Gospel.

2. A Book of Ethics

Then, secondly, this Gospel is also a book of ethics, showing us how to live; how to conduct ourselves. Once again, the other Gospels certainly do this also, but every writer and student of *Luke's Gospel* will immediately agree with the following assertion. Luke emphasises more definitely and more continuously than any other Gospel writer the tender love and helpfulness shown by our Lord and Saviour Jesus Christ to those who were down, and weak, and to women, children, and those who were despised.

Luke is pre-eminently the Gospel which brings before us Jesus Christ as a sympathetic high priest, telling us constantly that we too should have the same sympathy. It tells us how to live. We find this emphasis in phrases like: 'Love your enemies, do good to them which hate you, bless them that curse you, and pray for them which despitefully use you.' These phrases occur in *Luke 6.27-28*. While we have something similar in *Matthew 5.43-48*, we find such teaching in so concise a form only in *Luke's Gospel*.

In *Luke 7.36-50* there is the account, only found in *Luke*, of the sinful woman who comes to Jesus very sorry about her sin. As she goes to anoint Jesus, she breaks out in tears. These tears moisten the feet of Jesus, and she wipes them away with her hair.

But then we notice how Simon, the Pharisee, says to himself, 'This man, if he were a prophet, would have known who and what manner of woman this is that toucheth him: for she is a sinner.' Then Jesus, by means of the parable of the two debtors, exposes the heartlessness of the Pharisee, and he says to the woman, 'Thy sins are forgiven . . .

Thy faith hath saved thee; go in peace.' Here we have an example of how, at the same time, Jesus tells us all how to approach God, and how we should live; what our attitude should be toward those who are in need of our forgiveness and compassion.

And then you have the tenth chapter of *Luke* with the parable of the Good Samaritan or, if you wish, 'the Samaritan who cared'. While it certainly points to Christ, it also makes a clear ethical point. The Lord was asked by the legal expert, 'And who is my neighbour?' Did Jesus answer this man by telling him who his neighbour was? He did not. Just look at what the parable says toward the end. Jesus says, 'Which now of these three, thinkest thou, was neighbour unto him that fell among the thieves?'

In other words, Jesus really said to that legal expert, 'Do not ask – Who is my neighbour? You are the neighbour, and you must act as neighbour to whoever happens to settle in your path for your help.' Once again, therefore, we see that Luke relays the message of how we should live, and how greatly we need to be shown this. Is it not true that once in a while we find ourselves praying rather superficially along these lines: 'Oh God, bless everyone'? It is so easy to fall into such ways.

> *I knelt in prayer when day was done,*
> *And prayed, 'Oh God, bless everyone,*
> *Lift from their hearts the load of pain;*
> *And may the sick get well again.'*
> *I slept, and then another day,*
> *And carelessly I went my way.*
>
> *The whole day long I did not try*
> *To wipe a tear from any eye.*
> *I did not try to ease the load*
> *Of any sufferer on the road.*
> *I did not even go to see*
> *That sick man right next door to me.*
>
> *Then once again when day was done I prayed,*
> *'Oh God, bless everyone.'*
> *But as I prayed, unto my ear,*

There came a voice that whispered clear,
'Stop, hypocrite! Before you pray,
Who did you try to bless today?

'God's choicest blessings always go,
To those who serve Him here below.'
Ashamed, I hid my face and cried,
'Forgive me, Lord, for I have lied.
Let me but live another day,
And I will live the way I pray.'

Author unknown

3. A Book of Comfort

There are, of course, many other examples of ethical teaching in this Gospel, but our third point is that *Luke's Gospel* is a book of comfort, showing us why we should rejoice. I do not know whether it has ever struck you, but the *Gospel of Luke* is unique in that it begins with five songs. There is the song of the angels, the song of Elisabeth, the song of Mary, the song of Zacharias and the song of Simeon. And the book ends in the same way, with rejoicing and praise. The disciples come away from the hill from which Christ had ascended, and Luke says that they returned with great rejoicing and were continually in the Temple, praising God.

In the fifteenth chapter, we find mention of joy in Heaven (and there is the greatest joy-story of all). When I think of Luke, with all the joy which runs through his Gospel, I cannot help thinking also of Paul, his good and intimate friend. Paul sings his way right through *Philippians*, and even says – Rejoice! rejoice! rejoice! again and again. It is the same with Luke.

Why all this joy? I confess to you that more than once, when I have read of the tremendously tender love of God revealed in the fifteenth chapter of *Luke*, I have had tears in my eyes. Indeed, I have been hardly able to expound it, because it puts us all to shame.

Let us picture for a moment the prodigal son. (I like the term 'lost son' much better.) Let us picture him coming back, his head hanging down. He looks dishevelled, and has bare and very sore feet. He is repentant; he is very sorry. He has composed a little speech which he is going to make to his father. 'Father, I have sinned against heaven, and before thee, and am no more worthy to be called thy son: make me as one of thy hired servants.'

Then his father sees him from afar, and the incident becomes so beautiful. We read that his father was filled with sympathy. His father's heart went out to him. And then, we notice, it says that his father ran. Now remember that this is not just an interesting story, like a bedtime story one might tell to children. Remember that the father represents the heavenly Father. As the father runs, we notice (and this is evident from a careful reading of the parable) some of his servants run also, because they are with him when he speaks.

Then the father falls on the neck of his son and kisses him again and again, fervently. The son begins to recite the speech he has composed, 'Father, I have sinned against heaven, and in thy sight, and am no more worthy to be called thy son.' But before he has a chance to complete his words, the father speaks. He does not want to hear any more. It is enough. He is already speaking to his servants. According to the Greek the father says – 'Bring forth the garment, the best one.' The adjective is placed after the noun, to emphasise the point. When, for example, we speak of a home as 'a beautiful home' we mean that it is a nice home. But if we were to call it 'the home beautiful', then we would be trying to convey that it was the ultimate example of beauty. Here in *Luke's Gospel* the robe is the best one – the premier robe. 'Put it on him,' says the father, 'and put a ring on his hand, and shoes on his feet: and bring hither the fatted calf, and kill it; and let us eat, and be merry: for this my son was dead, and is alive again; he was lost, and is found.'

We must remember that Jesus told this parable partly to show the Pharisees that there is joy in Heaven. This does not just mean that there is joy among the angels. Yes, the angels are included, but the joy is in the heart of God over even one sinner who repents. When we meet people who are burdened with their sins, and wonder whether God will accept them, we must point them to this beautiful parable, and tell them that God truly delights in the return of sinners, and has no pleasure in the death of the wicked.

What always grips me is what follows in the parable. People seem to think that the last part about the other brother might as well have been left out, but this is very important too. Notice how this very austere, selfish, older brother is treated by the father. The older brother, when he notices that there are festivities going on, does not even want to go into the house because he is so angry and jealous.

In such circumstances we might be inclined to say – If you do not want to come in, you just stay outside. But that is not the way that Jesus tells the parable. The father comes out, and the elder brother says, 'Lo, these many years do I serve thee, neither transgressed I at any time thy commandment: and yet thou never gavest me a kid, that I might make merry with my friends.' Then the father says, 'Son, thou art ever with me, and all that I have is thine. It was meet that we should make merry, and be glad: for this thy brother was dead, and is alive again; and was lost, and is found.'

Surely the language of the father is marvellous. And when we read *Genesis 4* we notice the kindly way God spoke to Cain when He warned him not to commit the sin he was thinking of committing. In such passages as these we have insight into the tremendously loving heart of our God, a theme caught by the lines of the following hymn:–

> There were ninety and nine that safely lay
>   In the shelter of the fold:
> But one was out in the hills away,
>   Far off from the gates of gold:
> Away in the mountains wild and bare,
> Away from the tender Shepherd's care.
>
> 'Lord, Thou hast here Thy ninety and nine,
>   Are they not enough for Thee?'
> But the Shepherd made answer: 'This of Mine

Has wandered away from Me,
And although the road be rough and steep,
I go to the desert to find My sheep.'

But none of the ransomed ever knew
*   How deep were the waters crossed;*
Nor how dark was the night that the Lord passed through,
*   Ere He found His sheep that was lost:*
Out in the desert He heard its cry,
Sick and helpless and ready to die.

And all through the mountains, thunder-riven,
*   And up from the rocky steep,*
There arose a glad cry to the gate of Heaven,
*   'Rejoice, I have found My sheep!'*
And the angels echoed around the throne,
'Rejoice, for the Lord brings back His own!'

Elizabeth C. Clephane
1830-1869

A special feature of *Luke's Gospel* is its comforting nature, communicating so wonderfully the tender love of our God.

4. A Book of Prophecy

Then, finally, the Gospel is surely a book of prophecy, informing us what to expect. I do not mean that *Luke* has more references to the prophets than some of the other Gospels, because *Matthew* certainly has many more. But there are some prophecies in *Luke* which are peculiar to *Luke*, and of which we must take heed.

There is, for example, *Luke 12.47-48* where Jesus says – 'And that servant, which knew his lord's will, and prepared not himself, neither did according to his will, shall be beaten with many stripes. But he that knew not, and did commit things worthy of stripes, shall be beaten with few stripes.' How often we forget this. If we want to be true to this passage, we must remember that even in hell there will be a great diversity in degrees of punishment. Some receive many stripes, and some fewer stripes.

And then there is another passage, *Luke 12.37*, which we should read again and again, and pray about, for it brings home the love of God so marvellously that we cannot thank Him enough for this passage. We read – 'Blessed are those servants, whom the lord when he cometh shall find watching.' (I prefer the translation – 'on the alert'.)

Some people may think that Jesus pronounces a special blessing upon those believers who just stand still, doing nothing useful for their Lord, but just looking to Heaven for His return, but that is not the point at all. The blessing is for those who are found on the alert; in other words it means that we have to be up and doing. But to finish the prophecy – 'Blessed are those servants whom the Lord, at His coming, will find on the alert. I solemnly declare to you that the Lord will dress Himself to serve, and will have them recline at the table, and He [personally] will come up and wait on them.'

Can we grasp this? Our Lord actually says that He loves us so much, that if we are faithful in His service, He will have us recline at the banqueting table of Heaven, and He will come and wait on us Himself. Perhaps someone thinks I have forgotten that the language of the Lord is symbolic language, and that it is only figurative. What is my answer to that? It is this: My brother or sister, make your point again. You are right, and I like to hear you say it. Tell me again that this beautiful verse is only a symbol, for this means that the reality will be far more wonderful, praise be to God!

Here, then, in *Luke's Gospel*, is instruction on doctrine, instruction about how to live, instruction which helps us to rejoice, and promises for the future.

4
The Heavenly Jerusalem
A Survey of Revelation

THE APOSTLE JOHN was in exile for his faith on the island of Patmos. It is a Sunday. Picture him, in your imagination, walking on the shores of that island. Is he perhaps longing to see again the friends whom he left in Ephesus? Is his soul yearning to be reunited with them? The billows booming on the shores do not satisfy his longing, nor do the mountains dimly silhouetted against the sky answer his yearning. Then suddenly it seems as if the distant horizon recedes. John is in the Spirit.

He hears, but not with physical ears. He sees, but not with physical eyes. He is in the Spirit, and every avenue of his soul is in direct communion with God. In this state he hears a voice, a loud voice, behind him. When he hears that voice (he is in the Spirit remember) he turns to see the speaker, and then, O, what a rush of memories and rapture of surprise, for he sees that same Lord Jesus Christ in Whose bosom he had once rested. But he sees Him now in an entirely different way. He sees Him in this vision –

' . . . clothed with a garment down to the foot, and girt about the paps with a golden girdle. His head and his hairs were white like wool, as white as snow; and his eyes were as a flame of fire; and his feet like unto fine brass, as if they burned in a furnace; and his voice as the sound of many waters. And he had in his right hand seven stars: and out of his mouth went a sharp twoedged sword: and his countenance was as the sun shineth in his strength.'

Christ, in this vision, is walking among the seven lampstands, and toward the end of the chapter we are given a little commentary, namely: that the stars which the Lord holds in His right hand are the angels of the churches, the messengers or ministers as we would say today, and the lamps themselves represent those churches. Immediately, therefore, we are given a key to the interpretation of the *Book of Revelation*. Those good people who say that everything in this book has to be interpreted literally are in conflict with what the book itself says. It says that symbols are being used.

In the first eleven chapters of the *Book of Revelation* you have a symbolic picture of the struggle between the Church and the world, or between unbelief and faith. From chapters 4 to 7 you read about the symbol of the seven seals. Now it stands to reason that when the lamps, or churches, shine for Jesus, then the world gets angry and causes those churches to suffer. The willingness of a believer to suffer for Christ is sealed to his heart by the Holy Spirit, so that he has the testimony within him that he is a child of God.

This symbol of the seven seals is therefore very natural and appropriate. The fact that persecution is certainly implied here is confirmed at the fifth seal, when we see the souls beneath the altar crying, 'How long, O Lord?' They are believers who have been killed for the sake of Christ. So persecution is clearly the subject of the symbol.

In chapters 8-11 you find the symbol of the trumpets. Trumpets warn, so therefore these chapters are about judgements. The persecuting world is being warned by God's judgements in every age. There are judgements in these chapters for the earth, for the sea, for the rivers and the fountains; also for the sun, the air, and the battlefield. These seven trumpet warnings do not speak of events that will happen in history, one after another. As soon as we begin to interpret the *Book of Revelation* in that way, we will become completely lost. It is simply that the lampstands, the seals, and also the trumpets, cover the entire earth.

The fact that these trumpets indicate God's answer to the persecution of His children is already made very clear at the beginning of the eighth chapter, for there the suffering saints of God in the midst of their persecution are seen sending their prayers as incense to Heaven. Incense is very often in Scripture a symbol of prayer. Then an angel comes and takes that censer, emptying it of its incense and filling it with fire, which is then cast on the earth. There are the thunderings and lightnings, in other words it is very clearly indicated that these trumpets of judgement are indeed the warning judgements. And these warning judgements occur all the time. They occur today, and it is a principle of history that they will continue until the end of time.

From chapter 12 we have something else, for here is the second vision of the *Book of Revelation*, and this is concerned with what lies behind the struggle (on earth) between the world and the Church. It is explained that the struggle between the Church and the world is actually a struggle between Christ (the Lamb) and Satan (who is often called the dragon in the *Book of Revelation*). In *Revelation 12* we are given the symbol of the woman who is about to bear a child. The dragon (meaning Satan, of course) stands in front of the woman, so that as soon as she gives birth, he may destroy the child.

This is so plain that it seems to me we do not need a minister to explain it to us. The symbolic language is easily understood because this is exactly what Satan wants to do; he wants to destroy the work of Christ, and, if he could, Christ Himself. But then you also read in *Revelation 12* that Satan did not succeed, and so (summarising history very quickly there) the child is taken up to God, unto His throne. And so it does not surprise us at all (through the following two chapters) that the dragon goes on to seek helpers.

He gets three helpers. The beast out of the sea is one. That is – the world's persecution aimed at the bodies of believers. The beast out of the earth is another, and this is also called the false prophet, a term which immediately gives the meaning to us. Together they represent the world as the centre of false prophecy, aiming to poison the minds of God's children. Babylon, the harlot, is the other helper, the centre of seduction, aiming to entice and seduce believers' hearts away from their Lord, and by this means to slay the children of God.

Moving through chapters 12-14, the vision starts with the beginning of the new dispensation and ends with judgement. Not all John's visions end with an obvious judgement scene, but most of them do and in the case of the others it is implied. So the visions cover the entire New Testament dispensation.

In chapters 15-16 you have the bowls of wrath. Now notice that here again it is quite easy to get the meaning because these bowls are now poured out. What is in these bowls? Wrath, which is poured out upon the wicked. In other words, in the trumpets you see the warning judgements, but if the people will not listen and if they are not converted, then the bowls of wrath are poured out upon them.

This happens, of course, every day of the week, all through the year and all over the world, as God says to souls, 'You have been warned, but you have not listened to these warnings, and so now the day of grace is over for you.' All who, having been often warned, harden their hearts, shall suddenly be destroyed, and that without mercy, as the Word of God says.

In chapters 17, 18 and 19 you read of Babylon, and then later *(Revelation 19.19-20)* of the beast and the false prophet. In other words that group of chapters is about the allies of the dragon, and how they are destroyed in the lake of fire, to be punished everlastingly. You see how skilfully the book is organised, for this now leaves only the dragon itself – Satan. And in the twentieth chapter Satan is dealt with.

Notice how in the twentieth chapter John sees (in his vision) an angel with the key of an abyss, also holding a great chain in his hand. The angel takes hold of the dragon, the old serpent, the devil, which is Satan, and casts him into the abyss. The angel shuts and seals the abyss in order that Satan may not be able to get out for a definite period, called here (symbolically) the thousand years. During this period Satan will not be able to deceive the nations.

Afterwards, you read, he must be let loose again for a little while. All this is quite easy to understand, for it is a description of the Gospel age. It does not mean that Satan is bound in every respect, for the Bible never teaches that. Satan is very much on the loose in a lot of respects. But in one respect he is bound, namely, 'that he should deceive the nations no more'. In other words, he is bound so that he will not be able to check the spread of the Gospel through all the nations throughout the whole Gospel period. This meant so much to the people of that day, when the Gospel had only been preached in a small part of the world, and had not virtually covered the earth as it has now.

We notice in the fourth verse of *Revelation 20* that John sees – 'the souls of them that were beheaded for the witness of Jesus, and for the word of God, and which had not worshipped the beast, neither his image, neither had received his mark upon their foreheads, or in their hands; and they lived and reigned with Christ a thousand years.' Now we must take that passage exactly as it is; we must not change it. It speaks of the *souls* of those believers. In other words, John is saying that while the Gospel age is taking place on earth, the souls of those who have already been killed for the sake of the Gospel are living and reigning with Christ in Heaven.

Then, in the eleventh verse, the judgement day comes next. So the thousand years precede the judgement day, and not the other way round. The eleventh and twelfth verses read:

'And I saw a great white throne, and him that sat on it, from whose face the earth and the heaven fled away; and there was found no place for them. And I saw the dead, small and great, stand before God; and the books were opened: and another book was opened, which is the book of life: and the dead were judged out of those things which were written in the books, according to their works.'

In other words, there we have a very clear picture of the final and universal judgement. This completes our brief review of the first 20 chapters of the *Book of Revelation*.

The Holy City

Now we may expand our study to consider 'Jerusalem the golden', the symbol or picture in chapters 21 and 22. Immediately we have another key verse to the interpretation of the *Book of Revelation*. It is verse 9 (and 10) of chapter 21.

'And there came unto me one of the seven angels which had the seven vials full of the seven last plagues, and talked with me, saying, Come hither, I will shew thee the bride, the Lamb's wife.'

The angel then took John along to a mountain great and high and showed him something which is the vital key to the interpretation of the vision. If we do not spot this we will get everything wrong. Remember that the angel had just said, 'Come with me and I will show you the bride, the wife of the Lamb,' but he took John to a mountain great and high and he showed him the holy city coming down from Heaven.

Was the angel deceiving John? Did he fail to fulfil his promise? Why did he promise the bride and instead show him a city? Surely no one would seriously suggest that the angel was telling a lie, or failing to keep his promise. The only conclusion you can draw is, of course, that the bride is the city. This is the key to understanding the city – it is another picture of the bride.

It must have been quite an experience for John to see what he now saw, and I would urge you to picture this in your mind, for it is a beautiful picture. Remember that it is not primarily a picture of Heaven. You cannot say, 'This is the way Heaven is going to look!' The angel said, 'I will show you the bride, the wife of the Lamb.'

Let us look at that wonderful, entrancing vision. The city which John saw in his vision measured 12,000 furlongs, which means about 1,500 miles, wide, long, and high – a perfect cube. In America we would just say – that means from Maine to Florida. Over here you might perhaps say – it means from London to Malta. But it was a perfect cube. And what was especially striking was that the city was of pure gold – pure, precious, shining, and yet transparent gold.

The streets (as verse 21 indicates) were of gold, and also, I suppose, most of the buildings. The walls also were at least partly of gold. Imagine a city of gold, stretching for all that length, all that breadth, and all that height! Those who interpret the whole *Book of Revelation* literally, think that this is a picture of a literal Jerusalem which will come down and land somewhere in Palestine. I do not know how it can fit into Palestine; I have never been able to understand that. But as long as we concentrate our mind on the idea that this is a vision, a symbol, then we can proceed safely.

These walls were great and high and the measurements are given. There were also foundations, or rather foundation-stones. These twelve stones must have been huge on account of the vast size of the city. These stones also presented a gorgeous display of scintillating splendour, for the colours were all different. There was the red sardius, the white jasper (which today we would call diamond), the blue sapphire, the green emerald, and so on. Try to visualise it. But what must have enhanced the sight for John, and impressed him very deeply, were the names (verse 14) inscribed on those foundation-stones.

You say, 'How could he see the foundation-stones if they were foundation-stones? He could not have seen them for they were at the bottom.' But John must be pictured as standing below the city, which was coming down from Heaven above. He was standing under it, and obviously a little bit to the side (otherwise it would have descended on top of him). From such a position he could certainly see those stones. And what did he see? He saw inscribed in each of these beautiful stones the name of an apostle of the Lamb, which, if we think a moment, means that he suddenly saw on one of them the name John, for he was one of the apostles of the Lamb.

There were also gates to the city, three to the east, three to the west, three to the north, and three to the south, all outer gates. Naturally a gate leads to a street, and all these streets would clearly lead toward the centre. Every gate was one pearl. Pearls as we know them are quite small, and even a very large one is usually rather smaller than an ordinary-sized marble. But each huge gate was one vast pearl, and all the gates were standing open wide. On these gates were written the names of the tribes of Israel.

Where did all those streets lead, coming from the east, the west, the north, and the south? They led to the object in the centre of the city, which was the throne of God. The verses of both chapters 21 and 22 refer to many people being in this city. 'Nations of them which are saved shall walk in the light of it: and the kings of the earth do bring their glory and honour into it.' But look particularly at chapter 22:

'And he shewed me a pure river of water of life, clear as crystal, proceeding out of the throne of God and of the Lamb.'

Perhaps you are acquainted with the little hymn, *Shall we gather at the river?* In that hymn is a line – 'The beautiful, beautiful river, that flows by the throne of God.' Every Pelagian and Arminian would say 'Amen!' to that, but no Calvinist would ever say that. The river does not of course flow *by* the throne, or no one would ever be saved. That little word 'by' should be changed to 'from', then the sentiment would be correct, for the river flows *from* the throne of God.

So then, we have that throne in the centre of the city, and the river flowing forth from it, and of course always branching out as the river of life always does. In *Psalm 46*, for example, we read: 'There is a river, the streams whereof shall make glad the city of God.' And so when that water flows out of the throne it branches out alongside each street, though not immediately bordering it.

Revelation 22.2 is a hard verse to translate, and perhaps the best translation is as follows: 'And between the street on this side and the river on that side there was the tree of life, bearing twelve crops of fruit, a fruit every month.' In other words, the picture is of a city which is full of fruits of life, every month a crop, there being no end to all these fruits.

This brings us to my last point – the meaning of all this. We have already seen that this city is a symbol or picture of the bride, and as everyone who knows even a little about the Bible is aware, the bride is the Church. I mean, of course, God's real Church – His elect people. There can be no doubt about that. How can there be another interpretation? Only if this is so did the angel fulfil his promise to show John the bride.

There are people who get disappointed when we come to this point. They think, 'Up to this time we thought this was pretty good. The speaker was telling us exactly how Heaven was going to look. And now he changes it all and says it is a picture of the Church.' And they are not so inspired about that.

Now, of course, if children want something, you have to give them something; and so I always tell them – You may be sure of this, that as far as Heaven is concerned, it is going to be at least as beautiful as I have already pictured this particular symbol. You need not be afraid of that. But that is not the meaning of the symbol.

I was so very glad that once, when I gave this talk, Professor Louis Berkhof was present. He had been my professor of theology, both of doctrine and exegesis. Professor Berkhof, who wrote the famous *Systematic Theology* which is still so widely used today, was a wonderful man. I was first a student under him, then later I was his colleague as a professor in the seminary. He came to me after the message and said, 'That is what I believe. That is correct. I have so often heard it differently, but that's it.'

We should be very happy about the fact that this is a symbol of the Church, and especially of the Church in glory, the perfect Church. When we look at the symbol from this angle, everything begins to fall into place. When you think of the fact that this is a city of gold – pure, beautiful, transparent and precious – the thought that occurs to you immediately is, how very precious are we also to God. As the Church, we are precious in God's eyes!

And when you notice these gates all standing wide, and these sturdy walls, then of course they remind you of the fact that the people of God are absolutely secure. No enemy can ever enter there. Let the gates stand open wide! Let the walls be sturdy! Our salvation is also sturdy in the eyes of God, for that which He has begun in us He will certainly also complete, until the very coming of Christ.

Then when you look at the foundation-stones you realise that the names of the apostles must be on these stones, because the writings of the apostles (and, by extension, also of the prophets of the Old Testament) are the foundation upon which the Church is built. In other words, the Church, the real Church of God, is based upon the foundation of the infallible Word.

The throne is in the centre of the city to emphasise that God is the author, the sovereign author, of our salvation. Everything is ruled by Him. That is also why the river has to flow out of the throne, the river of grace, of course, which makes possible the trees of everlasting life.

Let us look a little further at the vision of the city. What is this everlasting life indicated by the trees of life? Does it mean existence without end? No, that is not the fulness of the meaning. Everlasting life is defined again and again in Scripture. It is the light of the knowledge of the glory of God in the face of Jesus Christ, which is joy unspeakable and full of glory; the peace of God that passes all understanding; fellowship and communion with Jesus Christ! This is life eternal, that they know God and the One Whom He has sent, Jesus Christ. All of these glorious possessions go on and on for evermore – that is everlasting life. Let us see just how close that fellowship in everlasting life is, according to the *Book of Revelation*.

It has always struck me, as I have worked through the whole *Book of Revelation* verse by verse, how very close that sweetness of fellowship is. In as far as it is possible for a creature – and I always have to add that, because there always remains an infinite, qualitative difference between Christ and ourselves – in as far as it is possible for a creature, then wherever Christ is, we are; whatever He does, we do; whatever He receives, we receive. Let me establish what I mean.

In *Revelation 3.12* we read that when Jesus Christ receives a new name, He immediately writes that name upon the foreheads of His redeemed. He receives it, and so they must have it.

In *Revelation 14.1*, when Jesus Christ is symbolically pictured standing upon Mount Zion, we immediately read that the 144,000 were standing there with Him.

In *Revelation 14.14* we are told that Jesus Christ had a golden crown upon His head, and in *Revelation 4.4* we are similarly told that the four and twenty elders (symbolising the one Church of both Old and New Testaments – 12 patriarchs and 12 apostles) also had golden crowns upon their heads.

In *Revelation 19.11* and *14* we notice that Christ is the rider upon the white horse, and immediately we read that His servants followed Him on white horses. Is this not beautiful? Always, what He has, they have; what He does, they do.

In *Revelation 20.4* we read about Jesus Christ living and reigning and we read in that same verse that those Christians who are there in Heaven live and reign with Him.

And what I think is perhaps the most beautiful identification of all is to be found in *Revelation 3.21*. Where are we going to be? 'To him that overcometh will I grant to sit with me in my throne, even as I also overcame, and am set down with my Father in his throne.'

Think of the intimacy of the fellowship, the sweetness of our communion with Christ. It is so great and so intimate that when He sits upon the throne, we sit with Him on that throne. We would not dare to say it but the Bible says it in so many words.

I want to picture, last of all, that sweetness of fellowship in the symbolic language of the songs which are sung there, in the city of God's people, the perfected Church. In *Revelation* chapter 4 you read of the song of the four living creatures, the four cherubim, ranged around the throne: 'Holy, holy, holy, Lord God Almighty, which was, and is, and is to come.'

As they sing that song of adoration to the Father, the four and twenty elders join in with: 'Thou art worthy, O Lord, to receive glory and honour and power: for thou hast created all things, and for thy pleasure they are and were created.'

In the next chapter Christ ascends the throne with the Father (that is the picture of His glorification in Heaven) and then you read that the Church has a song and is singing to the honour of the Christ. And the Church, the living creatures and the four and twenty elders join their voices to sing to Christ:

'Thou art worthy to take the book *[that is, the book of the decree fulfilled in history]*, and to open the seals thereof: for thou wast slain, and hast redeemed us to God by thy blood out of every kindred, and tongue, and people, and nation; and hast made us unto our God kings and priests: and we shall reign on the earth.'

Then, and this seems to me to be one of the most sublime things in the *Book of Revelation*, we must picture row upon row, or circle upon circle of angels. Picture the most distant circle you can imagine, and then place another circle inside of that, and then another one inside of that and so on – until finally the circles nearly reach the centre. Then picture the throne which is in the centre. We read that there were ten thousands of ten thousands and thousands of thousands of angels, voices coming from the far distance and also coming from nearby, all united in adoration because they loved the

Lord so very much. All are singing in adoration:

'Worthy is the Lamb that was slain to receive power, and riches, and wisdom, and strength, and honour, and glory, and blessing.'

And then from everywhere, the whole redeemed creation, cherubim, seraphim, sang a song to the Father and the Son:

'Blessing, and honour, and glory, and power, be unto him that sitteth upon the throne, and unto the Lamb for ever and ever.'

And the song was so beautiful and so entrancing, that the four living creatures said, 'Amen.' And the elders, who represent us, as those who had to be redeemed by blood (remember that the angels did not need to be redeemed), were so moved that no words are recorded.

Have you ever experienced something which was so wonderful you had, as it were, a lump in your throat so that you could not express it? All we read is: 'And the four and twenty elders fell down and worshipped.' So marvellous is the love of God in Christ for His people, already experienced by us in principle, but so much more by and by, that the elders were moved beyond song.

And our God's gracious, wonderful invitation is seen again even in the last chapter of *Revelation* in verse 17:

'And let him that is athirst come. And whosoever will, let him take the water of life freely.'

Great Passages
from
William Hendriksen

THE FOLLOWING PAGES provide a number of gems from Dr Hendriksen's commentaries which may stand alone as defining statements on important themes, both doctrinal and devotionally stirring in character.

These passages may lead readers to see the very special value of Dr Hendriksen's commentaries, whether for message-preparers or more substantial devotional reading. (Scripture quotations are from the author's own translation. Greek terms and technical footnotes have been omitted.)

The author's *New Testament Commentary* volumes are published in the USA by Baker Book House, and in the UK by the Banner of Truth Trust (see end pages and www.banneroftruth.co.uk).

What is an Apostle?
Romans 1.1

Paul, a servant of Jesus Christ, called to be an apostle.

In determining the meaning of the term *apostle* here in Rom. 1:1 it will be far better to study those passages in which it is used in its more usual sense. Occurring ten times in the Gospels, almost thirty times in Acts, more than thirty times in the Pauline epistles (including the five occurrences in the Pastorals), and eight times in the rest of the New Testament, it generally (but note important exception in Heb. 3:1 and the exceptions already indicated) refers to the Twelve and Paul.

In that fullest, deepest sense a man is an apostle *for life* and *wherever he goes*. He is clothed with *the authority of* the One who sent him, and that authority concerns both *doctrine and life*. The idea, found in much present-day religious literature, according to which an apostle has no real office, no authority, lacks scriptural support. Anyone can see this for himself by studying such passages as Matt. 16:19; 18:18; 28:18, 19 (note the connection); John 20:23;

I Cor. 5:3-5; II Cor. 10:8; I Thess. 2:6. Paul, then, was an apostle in the richest sense of the term. His apostleship was the same as that of the Twelve. Hence, we speak of "the Twelve and Paul." Paul even stresses the fact that the risen Savior had appeared to *him* just as truly as he had appeared to Cephas (I Cor. 15:5, 8). That same Savior had assigned to him a task so broad and universal that his entire life was henceforth to be occupied with it (Acts 26:16-18).

Yet Paul was definitely *not* one of the Twelve. The idea that the disciples had made a mistake when they had chosen Matthias to take the place of Judas, and that the Holy Spirit later designated Paul as the real substitute, hardly merits consideration (see Acts 1:24). *But if he was not one of the Twelve yet was invested with the same office, what was the relation between him and the Twelve?* The answer is probably suggested by Acts 1:8 and Gal. 2:7-9. On the basis of these passages this answer can be formulated thus: The Twelve, by recognizing Paul as having been specially called to minister to the Gentiles, were in effect carrying out through him their calling to the Gentiles.

The characteristics of full apostleship – the apostleship of the Twelve and Paul – were as follows:

In the first place, the apostles have been chosen, called, and sent forth by Christ himself. They have received their commission directly from him (John 6:70; 13:18; 15:16, 19; Gal. 1:6).

Secondly, they are qualified for their tasks by Jesus, and have been ear-and-eye witnesses of his words and deeds; specifically, they are the witnesses of his resurrection (Acts 1:8, 21, 22; I Cor. 9:1; 15:8; Gal. 1:12; Eph. 3:2-8; I John 1:1-3). Note: though Acts 1:21, 22 does not apply to Paul, the other passages do apply to him. Paul too had seen the Lord!

Thirdly, they have been endowed in a special measure with the Holy Spirit, and it is this Holy Spirit who leads them into all the truth (Matt. 10:20; John 14:26; 15:26; 16:7-14; 20:22; I Cor. 2:10-13; 7:40; I Thess. 4:8).

Fourthly, God blesses their work, confirming its value by means of signs and miracles, and giving them much fruit upon their labors (Matt. 10:1, 8; Acts 2:43; 3:2; 5:12-16; Rom. 15:18, 19; I Cor. 9:2; II Cor. 12:12; Gal. 2:8).

Fifthly, their office is not restricted to a local church, neither does it extend over a short period of time; on the contrary, it is for the entire church and for life (Acts 26:16-18; II Tim. 4:7, 8).

Note "a *called* apostle." This surely is much better than either "called an apostle" or "called to be or to become an apostle." What the original means is that Paul was an apostle by virtue of having been effectively called by God to this office. Similarly the people he addresses were *saints* by virtue of having been called, "saints by (divine) vocation."

As a called apostle, Paul had been "set apart for the gospel of God." From the beginning he had been designed by God for the proclamation of the gospel. Note especially Gal. 1:15, where the apostle expresses himself as follows, ". . . it pleased him who separated me from my mother's womb and called me through his grace, to reveal his Son in me, in order that I might preach his gospel among the Gentiles. . . ."

Paul speaks of "the gospel *of God*" or "*God's* gospel." And it is indeed the God-spell, the *spell* or *story* that tells us what *God* has done to save sinners. For that very reason it is an *evangel* or *message of good tidings*. It is the glad news of salvation which God addresses to a world lost in sin.

The Salvation Chain
Romans 8.29

For whom he foreknew, he also foreordained to be conformed to the image of his Son, so that he might be the firstborn among many brothers.

When Paul states that to those who love God and are called according to his purpose all things work together for good, he is not thinking only of those things that can be seen round about us *now*, or those events that are taking place *now*; no, he includes even time and eternity. The chain of salvation he is discussing reaches back to that which, considered from a human standpoint, could be called the dim past, "the quiet recess of eternity," and forward into the boundless future.

One very important fact must be mentioned: every link in this chain of salvation represents a divine action. To be sure, human responsibility and action is not thereby ruled out, but here (Rom. 8:29, 30) it is never specifically mentioned.

There are five links in this chain. Note that the predicate of the first clause becomes the subject of the next one, a construction called *sorities*.

A. *Foreknowledge*

". . . whom he foreknew."

Is it possible to interpret Paul's words in this sense: Before the world was created God foresaw who were going to believe in him and who would not. So, on the basis of that foreseen faith, he decided to elect to salvation those good people who were going to exercise it?

Answer: such a construction is entirely impossible, for according to

Scripture even faith is God's gift. See Eph. 2:8; John 6:44, 65; I Cor. 4:7; Phil. 1:29. In fact, even the good works performed by believers are prepared beforehand by God! (Eph. 2:10).

On the contrary, the foreknowledge mentioned in Rom. 8:29 refers to *divine active delight*. It indicates that, in his own sovereign good pleasure, God set his love on certain individuals, many still to be born, gladly acknowledging them as his own, electing them to everlasting life and glory. Note the following:

"For I have known him [Abraham] so that he may direct his children and his household after him" (Gen. 18:19).

"Before I formed you in the womb I knew you, Before you were born I set you apart" (Jer. 1:5).

"I am the good shepherd, and I know my own" (John 10:14). Cf. 10:28.

"The Lord knows who are his" (II Tim. 2:19).

Add the following: Ps. 1:6; Amos 3:2; Hos. 13:5; Matt. 7:23; I Cor. 8:3; Gal. 4:9; I John 3:1; and see also on Rom. 11:2.

"The term *prognosis* [foreknowledge] reveals the fact that in his purpose according to election the persons are not the objects of God's 'bare foreknowledge' but of his 'active delight.'" (H. Bavinck, *The Doctrine of God.*)

B. *Foreordination with a View to Conformation*

". . . he also foreordained to be conformed to the image of his Son, so that he might be the firstborn among many brothers."

In reality "foreknowledge" already implies "foreordination." Nevertheless, there is a difference of emphasis. Whereas the first term directs our attention to the persons whom God elected and only in a general way to their final destiny (everlasting life, glory), the term *foreordination* fixes our thought more definitely on the purpose for which they were elected and on the means of attaining it. That goal is not just "to enter heaven at last" but "to be conformed to the image of God's Son."

Conflict in the Believer
Galatians 5.16-18

16. But I say, walk by the Spirit, and you will definitely not fulfil the desire of the flesh. Let your conduct be governed by the Spirit, that is, by God's gift imparted to you (3:2, 5). If you follow his directions and promptings you will not be dominated by your human nature regarded as the seat and vehicle of sinful desire (as in 5:13), but instead will conquer it. It takes the tender leaves of early springtime to rid the oak tree of the remnants of last autumn's withered foliage. It is only the living that can expel the dead. It is only the good that can push out the bad.

Verse 16 clearly implies that there is a conflict between the Spirit and the flesh, therefore also between the believer's new, Spirit-indwelt, nature and his old, sinful, self. Hence, Paul continues: **17. for the flesh sets its desire against the Spirit, and the Spirit against the flesh: for these are opposed to each other....** True, as long as one allows himself to be led by the Spirit he will definitely not fulfil the desire of the flesh, but how often does it not happen that the person in question does not allow the Spirit to be his Leader? And so, because the Spirit persists, a fierce conflict takes place inside the believer's heart. The antagonists are: the Spirit – hence also the Spirit-indwelt new nature – on the one side; and on the other side: the flesh, that is, "the old man" of sin and corruption (same meaning as in verses 13 and 19 of this chapter, and as in 6:8; cf. Rom. 7:25; 8:4-9, 12, 13).

In connection with this contest, note the following:

(1) The *libertine* experiences no such struggle at all, for he follows his natural inclinations.

(2) The *legalist*, who is destined for grace and glory, having been reminded of his sinfulness by the law but for a while unwilling to accept grace, struggles and struggles but without achieving victory or experiencing the sense of certain, ultimate triumph. This condition lasts until grace finally breaks down all the barriers of opposition (Phil. 3:7 ff.).

(3) The *believer*, while still on earth, experiences an agonizing conflict in his own heart, but *in principle*, has already gained the victory, as the very presence of the Holy Spirit in his heart testifies. In full measure this victory will be his portion in the hereafter; hence,

(4) For *the redeemed soul in glory* the battle is over. He wears the victor's wreath.

As to (3), therefore, the very wording of the text – note: "sets its desire against" and "are opposed to each other" – indicates the intensity of the lifelong tug of war . . . He does not leap into heaven in one prodigious bound. On the contrary, he has to *work out* his own salvation (Phil. 2:12). This takes time, struggle, intense effort and exertion. He is his own most powerful enemy, as Paul proves by continuing: **so that these very things which you may wish to be doing, these you are not doing.** What a battle between the will and the deed! Paul, writing as a converted man (Rom. 7:14-25) and recording his *present, "state of grace"* experiences (for proof see Rom. 7:22, 25), complains bitterly about the fact that he practises that in which his soul no longer takes delight; in fact, practises that which his regenerated self *hates* (Rom. 7:15). He cries out, "Wretched man that I am! Who will deliver me out of the body of this death?" (Rom. 7:24). Nevertheless, he is also fully aware of the fact that in the struggle between his own flesh and God's Spirit, the latter's victory – hence also Paul's – is certain; in fact, *in principle* is a fact even now. Would there have been this genuine, *God-centered* sorrow for sin, had not Paul been a truly converted man? Of course not! This very conflict, therefore, is a charter of the apostle's salvation. We are not surprised, therefore, that the exclamation "Wretched man! . . . Who will deliver me?" is followed by "I thank God through Jesus Christ our Lord. . . . There is therefore now no condemnation to them that are in Christ Jesus" (Rom. 7:25; 8:1; cf. I Cor. 15:57). Similarly here in Galatians the thought of victory through the Spirit is basic to the understanding of verse **18. But if you are being led by the Spirit you are not under law.** Being "under law" spells defeat, bondage, the curse, spiritual impotence, for the law cannot save (Gal. 3:11-13, 21-23, 25; 4:3, 24, 25; 5:1). It takes the Spirit to set one free (4:29; 5:1, 5; II Cor. 3:17).

Being Led by the Spirit

(1) *Whom It Concerns*

According to a rather popular view "spiritual leading" is the Spirit's gift to the select few, "the holiest men," the flower of the flock. It is imparted to them to protect them from physical harm, especially while traveling, to deliver them from dangerous situations, and sometimes even to insure them success in their business enterprises.

However, when, with Gal. 5:18 as our starting-point, we trace *back* the line of Paul's thinking, it becomes evident that this limitation of "spiritual leading" to a group of super-saints is completely foreign to his mind. Those who are being led by the Spirit (5:18) are the same as those who walk by the Spirit (5:16), and vice versa. Going back a little farther, we notice that these, in turn, are the ones who have been set free (5:1; 4:31, 26), who belong to Christ (3:29), and are "of faith" (3:9). All true believers, therefore, are being led by the Spirit.

Moreover, the powerful influence that is being exercised upon and within them by the Spirit is not of a sporadic character, being, as it were, injected into their lives now and then in moments of great need or danger. On the contrary, it is steady, constant, as even the tense here in Gal. 5:18 implies: they *are being led* by the Spirit. Even when they disobey the Spirit – and they certainly do, as has just been set forth (verses 13-17) – the Spirit does not leave them alone but works repentance within their hearts.

This representation is in keeping with the only other truly parallel passage in Paul's epistles, namely, Rom. 8:14: "For as many as are being led by the Spirit of God, these are sons of God." Here, too, being led by the Spirit is set forth as the indispensable characteristic of God's children. If a person is a child of God he is being led by the Spirit. If he is being led by the Spirit he is a child of God.

(2) *What It Is*

Before giving a positive answer to this question it may be well to point out what is *not* meant by being led by the Spirit. Naturally, it cannot refer to being governed by one's own sinful impulses and inclinations, nor to "being easily led" into waywardness by evil companions. Also definitely excluded here is the idea of those moral philosophers, ancient and modern, who hold that in every man there is a higher and a lower nature, and that each human being has within himself the power of causing the former to triumph over the latter. This idea is excluded even if for no other reason than this, that throughout, in Paul's teaching, the Holy Spirit is a distinct person, of one substance with the Father and the Son. He is not "our other or better self." See Rom. 8:26, 27; I Cor. 2:10; II Cor. 13:14. This also shows that, strictly speaking, being led by the Spirit cannot even be identified with the triumph of "the new man" (the regenerated nature) within us over "the old man" (our corrupt nature, not yet fully destroyed). That victory and that implied struggle are certainly very real; yet they are not *in and by themselves* what is meant by being led by the Spirit, but are rather *the result* of the Spirit's active indwelling. They are certainly *implied*, but are not basic.

What then does *the leading of the Spirit* – to change from the passive to the active voice, for the sake of the definition – actually mean? It means sanctification. *It is that constant, effective, and beneficent influence which the Holy Spirit exercises within the hearts of God's children whereby they are being directed and enabled more and more to crush the power of indwelling sin and to walk in the way of God's commandments, freely and cheerfully.*

Christ Dwelling in the Heart
Ephesians 3.16-19a

16, 17a. Paul has introduced his moving trinitarian prayer by saying, "For this reason I bend my knees to the Father, from whom the whole family in heaven and on earth derives its name: the Father's Family," and he continues, **(praying) that according to the riches of his glory he may grant you to be strengthened with power through his Spirit in the inner man, that Christ may dwell in your hearts through faith.** God is *glorious* in all his attributes. His power (1:19; 3:7) is infinite; his love (1:5; 2:4) is great; his mercy (1:4) and his grace (1:2, 6; 2:7, 8) are rich; his wisdom (3:10) is iridescent; etc. Note particularly such expressions as "the surpassing riches of his grace (expressed) in kindness" (2:7) and compare "the unfathomable riches of Christ" (3:8). In the work of salvation it is never right to stress one attribute at the expense of another. Hodge is right when he states, "It is not his power to the exclusion of his mercy, nor his mercy to the exclusion of his power, but it is everything in God that renders him glorious, the proper object of adoration." Paul prays therefore that all of God's resplendent attributes may be richly applied to the spiritual progress of those whom he addresses. In particular, he asks that the One who, as 1:19 (cf. 3:7, 20; Col. 1:11) has shown, is himself the Source of power in all its various manifestations, may grant to the Ephesians that, in accordance with the measure of God's glory, they may be strengthened with power through his Spirit in the inner man. This "inner man" is not that which is rational in man as contrasted with man's lower appetites. Paul's terminology is not that of Plato or of the Stoics. On the contrary, the "inner man" is the opposite of the "outer" (or: outward) man. Cf. II Cor. 4:16. The former is hidden from the public gaze. The latter is open to the public. It is in the *hearts* of believers that the principle of a new life has been implanted by the Holy Spirit. See 3:17. What the writer is praying for is therefore this, that within these hearts such a controlling influence may be exerted that they may be strengthened more and more with Spirit-imparted power. See 1:19; cf. Acts 1:8. Another way of putting the same thought is this: "that Christ may dwell in your hearts through faith." Wrong is the idea, rather popular among some commentators, that *first*, for a while, the Spirit imparts strength to believers, *after which* there arrives a time when Christ establishes his abode in these now strengthened hearts. Christ and the Spirit cannot be thus separated. When believers have the Spirit within themselves they have Christ within themselves, as is very clear from Rom. 8:9, 10. "In the Spirit" Christ himself inhabits the believers' inner selves. Cf. Gal. 2:20; 3:2. The heart is the mainspring of dispositions as well as of feelings and thoughts (Matt. 15:19; 22:37; Phil. 1:7; I Tim. 1:5). Out of it are the issues of life (Prov. 4:23). Christ's precious indwelling is "through faith," the latter being the hand that accepts God's gifts. Faith is full surrender to God in Christ, so that one expects everything from God and yields everything to him. It works through love (Gal. 5:6).

. . . The immediate purpose of the strengthening and the indwelling is stated in words which indicate, as it were, the second rung of this prayer-ladder: **17b-19a. in order that you, being rooted and founded in love, may be strong, together with all the saints, to grasp what is the breadth and length and height and depth, and to know the love of Christ that surpasses knowledge.** Since faith works through love, and amounts to nothing without it (I Cor. 13:2), it is easy to see that if *by faith* Christ has established his abiding presence in the heart, believers will be firmly rooted and founded *in love*, a love for God in Christ, for the brothers and sisters in the Lord, for the neighbors, even for enemies. Moreover, this love, in turn, is necessary in order to comprehend Christ's love for those who love him. And in the measure in which the believers' vision of that love which proceeds from Christ expands, their love for him and their ability to grasp his love for them will also increase, etc. Thus the most powerful and blessed chain-reaction in the whole universe is established. It all *began* with God's love in Christ for the Ephesians (1:4, 5; I John 4:19). Like a continuing circle it will *never end.*

The words "rooted and founded" suggest a twofold metaphor: that of *a tree* and that of *a building*. To insure the stability of the tree roots are required, roots that will be in proportion to the spread of the branches. Similarly, as a guarantee for the solidity of a building a foundation is necessary, one that will adequately support the super-structure. Thus firmly rooted the tree, which represents all those who love the Lord, will flourish and bear the indicated fruit. Thus solidly founded the building will continue to grow into a holy sanctuary in the Lord, and will achieve its purpose.

That fruit and purpose is "to grasp what is the breadth and length and height and depth, and to know the love of Christ." Since such *grasping* or *appropriating* and *knowing* can be practised only by those who are rooted and founded in *love*, it is clear that the reference is not to an activity that is purely mental. It is *experiential* knowledge, *heart*-knowledge, which Paul has in mind. And since the heart is the very core and center of life and influences all of life's inner activities and outward expressions, what is indicated is a grasping and a knowing with one's entire being, that is, with *all* the "faculties" of heart and mind. Mental appropriation is certainly *included*.

... The *Lofty Ideal* is to get to know *thoroughly* Christ's deep affection, self-sacrificing tenderness, passionate sympathy, and marvelous outgoingness. All of these are included in *love* but do not exhaust it. Paul prays that the addressed may appropriate and know this love in all its breadth and length and height and depth! Here, as I see it, the expositor should be on his guard. He should not pluck this expression apart, so that a separate meaning is ascribed to each of these dimensions. What is meant is simply this: Paul prays that the Ephesians (and all believers down through the centuries) may be so earnest and zealous in the pursuit of their objective that they will never get to the point where they will say, "We have arrived. *Now* we know all there is to know about the love of Christ." Just as Abraham was told to look toward heaven and number the stars, so that he might see that numbering them was impossible; and just as we today are being urged by means of a hymn to count our many blessings, and to name them one by one, so that their uncountable multitude may increase our gratitude and astonishment, so also the apostle prays that the addressed may concentrate so intensely and exhaustively on the immensity and glory of Christ's love that they will come to understand *that this love ever surpasses knowledge.* The *finite* heart and mind can never fully grasp or know *infinite* love. Even in the life hereafter God will never say to his redeemed, "Now I have told you all there is to be told about this love. I close the book, for the last page has been read." There will always be more and more and still more to tell. And that will be the blessedness of the heavenly life.

A Husband's Love
Ephesians 5.32

Paul adds: **32. This mystery is great, but I am speaking with reference to Christ and the church.** Paul has just now spoken about the marriage ordinance, in accordance with which *two* people become so intimately united that in a sense they become *one.* "*This mystery* is great," he says. He must, therefore, be referring to marriage. However, he makes very clear that he is not thinking of marriage *in and by* *itself.* He definitely mentions once more the link between it and the Christ-church relationship. Accordingly, I can find no better answer to the question, "What is meant here by *the mystery,* that is, by *the secret that would have remained hidden had it not been revealed?*" than the one given by Robertson in his *Word Pictures, Vol. IV,* p. 547: "Clearly Paul means to say that the comparison of marriage to the union of Christ and the church is the mystery." The union of Christ with the church, so that, from the sweep of eternal delight in the presence of his Father, God's only begotten Son plunged himself into the *dreadful darkness and awful anguish of Calvary* in order to save his *rebellious people,* gathered from among all the nations, and even to dwell in their hearts through his Spirit and at last to present *them* – even these utterly undeserving ones – to himself as his own bride, with whom he becomes united in such intimate fellowship that no earthly metaphor can ever do justice to it, *this* even in and by itself is a mystery. Cf. 3:4-6; Col. 1:26, 27. But the fact that this marvelous love, this blissful Christ-church relationship, is actually reflected here on earth in the union of a husband and his wife, so that by the strength of the former bond (Christ-church), the latter (husband-wife) is now able to function most gloriously, bringing supreme happiness to the marriage-partners, blessing to mankind, and glory to God *that,* indeed, is the Mystery Supreme!

This idea of marriage should never be lost sight of by those who have been united in Christian matrimony. Every day the husband should ask himself, "Does my love for my wife reveal the marks of Christ's love for his church?" That high ideal must never be relinquished.

On Isaiah 53
(from Commentary on Philippians)

Between the evangel of the old dispensation and that of the new there is a very close connection. Thus, for example, apart from Isaiah 53 the New Testament cannot be understood:

When John the Baptist proclaimed his gospel, pointing to Jesus as the Lamb of God who takes away the sin of the world, was he not thinking of Isaiah 53? (John 1:29; cf. Isa. 53:7, 10).

When Matthew referred to Christ's humble origin and the lowly conditions of his birth, was there not a clear reference to Isaiah 53? (Matt. 2:23; cf. Isa. 11:1; 53:2).

When this same Matthew-passage and also many other New Testament references showed that Christ was despised, was not this in fulfilment of Isaiah 53? (Matt. 2:23; Luke 18:31-33; 23:35, 36; John 1:46; I Peter 2:4; cf. Isa. 53:3).

When John, the apostle and evangelist, summarized Israel's reaction to Christ's earthly ministry, did he not do it in words taken from Isaiah 53? (John 12:36-38; cf. Isa. 53:1).

When Jesus healed the sick, gave himself a ransom "for many," and "was reckoned with the transgressors," did he not fulfil Isaiah 53? (Matt. 8:16, 17; cf. Isa. 53:4; Matt. 20:28; Mark 10:45; cf. Isa. 53:11, 12; Luke 22:37; cf. Isa. 53:12).

When Matthew stated, "And there came a rich man and asked for the body of Jesus," was he not thinking of Isaiah 53? (Matt. 27:57; cf. Isa. 53:9).

When Jesus stressed that he regarded not only his suffering and death but also his entrance into glory (resurrection, etc.)

as fulfilment of prophecy, was he not thinking of a series of Old Testament passages which included Isaiah 53? (Luke 24:25, 26; cf. Isa. 53:10-12).

When Philip *the evangelist* told the Ethiopian eunuch the evangel or good news of Jesus, was not his text taken from Isaiah 53? (Acts 8:32, 33; cf. Isa. 53:7, 8).

When Peter described Christ's sinlessness and vicarious suffering for his wandering sheep, did he not do so in the very terms of Isaiah 53? (I Peter 2:22-25; cf. Isa. 53:4, 5, 6, 9, 12).

When the author of Hebrews dwelt on Christ's self-sacrifice for many, was not his source Isaiah 53? (Heb. 9:28; cf. Isa. 53:12).

When to John on Patmos the Lamb revealed himself in visions, was it not *the slaughtered Lamb* of Isaiah 53? (Rev. 5:6, 12; 13:8; 14:5; cf. Isa. 53:7).

And so also when Paul proclaimed what he delighted to call "my gospel," did he not base it on God's glorious redemptive revelation found in principle even in the Old Testament, and did he not include Isaiah 53 among his sources? (Rom. 4:25; I Cor. 15:3; cf. Isa. 53:5; Rom. 10:16; cf. Isa. 52:7; 53:1). *Note that not a single verse of Isa. 53 is ignored in the New Testament!*

The *evangel of the new dispensation is that of the old dispensation, gloriously amplified.* The gospel of the Coming Redeemer is transformed into the gospel of the Redeemer who came, who is coming again, and who imparts salvation, full and free, *to every believer on a basis of perfect equality.*

The Loss of All Things
Philippians 3.7-8

Nevertheless, such things as once were gains to me these have I counted loss.

7, 8a. In the two preceding verses Paul has enumerated his superior advantages as a genuine Israelite, of noble birth, orthodox in his belief, and scrupulous in his conduct. By means of these advantages the apostle, in his pre-conversion period, had been "bleeding to climb to God." But had it not been a case of

> "Gaining a foothold bit by bit
> Then slipping back and losing it"?

Worse even, for never at all had there been any *real* progress, no matter how hard he, Paul the Pharisee, had labored to establish his own righteousness. But on the way to Damascus to persecute Christians the great event occurred which changed his entire life. Christ, as it were, came down the stairs to him (read the gripping account in Acts 9:1-31; 22:1-21; 26:1-23). In a moment Paul saw himself as he really was, a deluded, self-righteous, damnable sinner. Then and there he embraced the One whom until now he had been persecuting with might and main. He became "a new creature." In his mind and heart he experienced a complete turn-about, a sudden and dramatic reversal of all values. The cause which with every means at his disposal and with all the zeal of heart and will he had been trying to wipe out now became very dear to him. And also, those things which to *Paul, the Pharisee,* had seemed very precious *became* at this moment – and ever after *remained* – useless to *Paul, the sinner, saved by grace;* and not merely *useless* but definitely *harmful.* Writes Paul,

Nevertheless, such things as once were gains to me these have I counted loss. Not that any of these things which he enumerated in verses 5 and 6, and other things like them, were bad in themselves. Quite the contrary. To receive the sign of the covenant is not bad in itself. It is, in fact, a blessing. And was it not a blessing to belong to that people to which the oracles of God had been entrusted? Orthodoxy, too, is in itself a good thing. So is zeal, and so certainly also is irreproachable conduct. Paul himself elsewhere informs us that he considers such things as these to be blessings (Rom. 3:1, 2; 9:1-5; cf. 11:1). They are blessings because they can be of inestimable value if properly used, namely, as a preparation for the reception of the gospel. But when these same privileges begin to be viewed as a basis for self-satisfaction and self-glorification, when they are regarded as a ticket to heaven, they are changed into their opposites. All these separate *gains* become *one huge loss.* This is Paul's deliberate, considered judgment. He considered the gains, and counted them loss. And in that judgment he persisted, as is implied in the tense of the Greek verb. On his balance-sheet those things which once were included, one by one, in the column of *assets* have now been transferred to the column of *liabilities,* and have been entered as *one gigantic liability.* Note that the plusses have not become a zero (0), but have become even less than zero, that is, one colossal MINUS (-). "For what will it profit a man if he gains the whole world and forfeits his life?" (Matt. 16:26; cf. Mark 8:36).

The word *loss* which Paul uses here in verses 7 and 8, and nowhere else in his epistles, occurs in only one other New Testament chapter, Acts 27 (verses 10 and 21), in the story of The Voyage Dangerous. And it is exactly that same chapter which also indicates how *gain* may become *loss.* The cargo on that ship bound for Italy represented potential *gain* for the merchants, for the owner of the ship, and for hungry people. Yet, had not this wheat been thrown into the sea (Acts 27:38), *loss,* not only of the ship but even of all those on board, might well have been the result. Thus also, the advantage of being born in a Christian home and having received a wonderful Christian home-training, becomes a disadvantage when it is viewed as a basis upon which to build one's hope for eternity. The same holds with respect to money, the charming look, a college education, physical strength, etc. All such helps may become hindrances. The stepping-stones will be turned into stumbling blocks, if wrongly used.

When the question is asked, "Why was it that, in Paul's considered judgment, these gains had become a loss?" the answer is **for Christ**, that is, for the sake of Christ; for, had Paul been unwilling to renounce his former estimate of these privileges and achievements, they would have deprived him of Christ, the one real gain (see verse 8).

Paul continues, in a sentence that is almost untranslatable, **Yes, what is more, I certainly do count all things to be sheer loss because of the all-surpassing excellence of knowing Christ Jesus my Lord.**

In verse 8 Paul strengthens his previous statement, and this in two ways. First, he underscores what was implied in the preceding, namely, that what he counted loss at the moment of his conversion he is still counting to be loss. It is as if he were saying, "On this subject no Judaizer will ever be able to change my mind." Secondly, he now affirms that he considers not only the things mentioned in verses 5 and 6 to be a liability, a detriment, but also all other things that could stand in the way of fully accepting Christ and his righteousness. We may think of such matters as making too much of earthly possessions, delight in intimate fellowship with former anti-Christian friends, anticipation centered on even more brilliant prospects as a Pharisee, etc. All such matters and many more are nothing but sheer loss, and this *because of* – hence also in *comparison with* – the all-surpassingness, that is, the all-surpassing excellence or value, of "knowing Christ Jesus … Lord." On the way to Damascus Paul had learned to know Jesus. Although there had been ample preparation for this knowledge – such as, Paul's acquaintance with the Old Testament, the testimonies he had heard from the lips of the martyrs, their behavior under fire – when it broke in upon the soul, the experience was sudden and dramatic. Prophecy and testimony began to take on meaning now. It was an unforgettable experience, that meeting with the exalted Christ, while, a moment before, the apostle had still been breathing threatening and slaughter against Christ's Church, hence against this very Christ himself! Yes, he now *saw and heard* the actual Jesus, about whom he had been told so much. And he saw and heard him now as *Christ Jesus ... Lord,* the name above every name (see 2:9-11). And at the same time he here and now began to understand something of the condescending pity and tenderness of Christ's great and merciful heart, a love poured out upon *him,* even upon *Paul, the bitter persecutor!*

All this had occurred about thirty years ago. And during the period that intervened between the "Great Experience" and the writing of the present epistle to the Philippians, the joy of knowing, with a knowledge of both mind and heart (see verse 10), *Christ Jesus ... Lord* had been growing constantly, so that it outshone everything in beauty and desirability. Hence, Paul inserts a little word which makes "that beautiful name, that wonderful name, that matchless name" of Jesus even more adorable. He says "Christ Jesus *my* Lord." What this appropriating *my* implies is better explained by Paul himself. Read Phil. 1:21; 4:13; Rom. 7:24, 25; II Cor. 12:8-10; Gal. 1:15, 16; 2:20; 6:14; Eph. 5:1, 2; Col. 3:1-4:6; I Tim. 1:5, 16; II Tim. 1:12; 4:7, 8. According to these passages Christ Jesus is much more than Paul's Example and Friend. He is his Life, Lover, Strength, Boast, Rock, Rewarder, and especially as here, his Anointed Savior and Sovereign.

As before the rising sun the stars fade out, and as in the presence of the pearl of great price all other gems lose their luster, so fellowship with "Christ Jesus my Lord" eclipses all else. And it is Christ himself of whom Paul is thinking, not this or that matter about Christ. Paul is in complete agreement with the poet who said, (not *"What"* but) *"Whom* have I in heaven but thee? And there is none on earth that I desire besides thee" (Ps. 73:25). The apostle continues, **for whom I suffered the loss of all these things.** It was for the sake of his Lord and Savior that Paul had lost whatever was at one time very dear to him: pride of tradition, of ancestry, of orthodoxy, of outward conformity with the law, and of whatever else there had been on which he had formerly depended as gateways to the heavenly city. Moreover his attitude of having willingly suffered this loss has not changed at all. So he continues, **and I am still counting them refuse.** What the Judaizers prize so very highly, the apostle considers to be nothing but *refuse,* something that is fit only to be thrown to the *dogs.* The apostle is very consistent. Had he not, just a moment ago (see 3:2), called these dangerous enemies *dogs?* Paul, then, considers all these inherited privileges and human attainments, *considered as merits,* to be something that must be discarded as worthless leavings, abominable trash.

Continuous Rejoicing
Philippians 4.4-7

4 Rejoice in the Lord always; again I will say, Rejoice. 5 Let your big-heartedness be known to everybody. The Lord (is) at hand. 6 In nothing be anxious, but in everything by prayer and supplication with thanksgiving let your petitions be made known before God. 7 And the peace of God that surpasses all understanding will keep guard over your hearts and your thoughts in Christ Jesus.

4:4-6, The Secret of True Blessedness:
A. What to Do to Obtain It

(1) Let joy reign *within*

4. Once again, as so often before, the apostle stresses the duty of rejoicing. He says, **Rejoice in the Lord always; again I will say, Rejoice.** The exhortation is repeated, probably because on the surface it seems so unreasonable to rejoice *in obedience to a command,* and perhaps even more unreasonable to rejoice *always,* under all circumstances no matter how trying. Can one truly rejoice when the memory of past sins vexes the soul, when dear ones are suffering, when one is being persecuted, facing possible death? But there is Paul, who does, indeed, remember his past sins (Phil. 3:6; cf. Gal. 1:13; I Cor. 15:9), whose friends are really suffering (Phil. 1:29, 30), who is even now a prisoner facing possible death; yet, who rejoices and tells others to do likewise! It is evident from this that circumstances alone do not determine the condition of heart and mind. A Christian can be joyful *within* when *without* all is dark and dreary. He rejoices *in the Lord,* that is, because of his oneness with Christ, the fruit of whose Spirit is *joy* (Gal. 5:22). This is reasonable, for in and through Christ all things – also those that seem most unfavorable – work together for good (Rom. 8:28).

It was not unreasonable for Paul *to exhort* the Philippians to rejoice, for the disposition of joy can be and should be cultivated. This can be done, as the apostle indicates in the context (see verse 8), by meditating on the proper subjects, that is, by taking account of the things that should stand out in our consciousness. For Paul such reasons for joy, the joy unspeakable and full of glory, were the following: that he was a saved individual whose purpose was in his entire person to magnify Christ (1:19, 20); that this Savior, in whose cross, crown, and coming again he glories (2:5-11; 3:20, 21; 4:5), was able and willing to supply his every need (4:11-13, 19, 20); that others, too, were being saved (1:6; 2:17, 18), the apostle himself being used by God for this glorious purpose; that he had many friends and helpers in the gospel-cause, who together formed a glorious *fellowship* in the Lord (1:5; 2:19-30; 4:1, 10); that God was causing all things, even bonds, to work together for good (1:12-18; cf. Rom. 8:28), so that even death is gain when life is Christ (1:21, 23); and that at all times he has freedom of access to the throne of grace (4:6). Let the Philippians meditate on these things and rejoice, yes rejoice *always*.

5a. (2) Let big-heartedness be shown *all around*.

A Christian should cultivate an outgoing personality. The secret of his happiness is not confined within the walls of his own meditation and reflection. He cannot be truly happy without striving to be a blessing to others. Hence, Paul continues, **Let your big-heartedness be known to everybody.** For *big-heartedness* one may substitute any of the following: forbearance, yieldedness, geniality, kindliness, gentleness, sweet reasonableness, considerateness, charitableness, mildness, magnanimity, generosity. All of these qualities are combined in the adjective-noun that is used in the original. Taken together they show the real meaning. When each of these would-be-English-equivalents is taken by itself alone, it becomes clear that there is not a single word in the English language that fully expresses the meaning of the original.

The lesson which Paul teaches is that true blessedness cannot be obtained by the person who rigorously insists on whatever he regards as his just due. The Christian is the man who reasons that it is far better to *suffer* wrong than to *inflict* wrong (I Cor. 6:7). Sweet reasonableness is an essential ingredient of true happiness. Now such big-heartedness, such forbearance, the patient willingness to yield wherever yielding is possible without violating any real principle, must be shown *to all*, not only to fellow-believers.

This Christian magnanimity probably stands in very close connection with the comfort which the Christian derives from the coming of the Lord, which coming has already been mentioned (Phil. 3:20, 21) and is about to be mentioned once more (4:5b, "the Lord is at hand"). The idea seems to be: since Christ's coming is near, when all the promises made to God's people will become realities, believers, in spite of being persecuted, can certainly afford to be mild and charitable in their relation to others.

5b, 6. (3) Let there be no worry but prayerful trusting in God *above.*

Joy *within*, big-heartedness *all around*, and now prayerful trusting in God *above.* Says Paul, **The Lord (is) at hand.** In view of the immediate context (3:20, 21) the meaning is probably not, "The Lord is always nearby or present," (cf. Ps. 145:18) but rather, "The Lord is coming very soon." This, of course, is strictly true with respect to every believer. If the Lord arrives from heaven before the believer dies, then no one surely will be able to doubt that this coming was, indeed, *at hand.* But if the death of the believer occurs before the day of Christ's coming, then two facts remain true both for the believer's own consciousness and according to the clear teaching of Scripture: a. The believer's life-span here on earth was very, very brief. In fact, it amounted to a mere breath (Ps. 39:5; 90:10; 103:15, 16); and b. the interval between the entrance of his soul into heaven and the Lord's second coming was but "a little season" (Rev. 6:11), for in heaven he was geared to a different kind of time-scale. Hence, take it either way, Paul had every right to say, "The Lord (is) at hand." Whatever happens in history is a preparation for this coming, which, as has been shown, will in either case be *soon.* This does not mean that the apostle excludes the possibility that *by earthly reckoning* there could still be an interval of many years before the Lord's arrival. He is not setting any dates (see I Thess. 5:1-3; II Thess. 2:1-3). In view of the fact that no one knows the day and the hour when Jesus will return (Matt. 24:36), it behooves every one to be ready, working, watching at all times (Matt. 25:1-13). At the coming of the Lord all wrongs will be righted, and the believer will stand in the presence of his Lord, fully vindicated. Hence, let him not make too much of disappointments, or unduly trouble himself about the future. So Paul continues, **In nothing be anxious** or "stop being anxious about anything." There is such a thing as *kindly concern*, that is, *genuine* *interest* in the welfare of others. The verb (used in Phil. 4:6, and here rendered "be anxious") can elsewhere have a favorable meaning, as it does, in fact, in this very epistle (2:20): Timothy *was genuinely interested* in the welfare of the Philippians. Often, however, it indicates *to be unduly concerned about, to be filled with anxiety, to worry.* Such worry may be about food or drink or clothes or one's life-span or the future or words to be spoken in self-defense or even about "many things" (Matt. 6:25-28, 34; 10:19; Luke 10:41; 12:11). The cure for worry is prayer. Hence, the apostle continues, **but in everything by prayer and supplication with thanksgiving let your petitions be made known before God.**

The cure for worry is not *inaction.* If one wishes to plant a garden, build a house, make a sermon, or do anything else, he cannot attain his objective by prayer *alone.* There must be careful planning. There must be *reflection* leading to *action.* Paul is not forgetting this. In fact, the *reflection* is stressed in verse 8, the *action* in verse 9. On the other hand, however, it is also true that reflection and action without prayer would be futile. In fact so very important is prayer to the Christian that it is mentioned first of all (verse 6b).

Neither is the cure for worry *apathy.* God never tells us to suppress every desire. On the contrary, he says, "Open your mouth wide, and I will fill it" (Ps. 81:10). Proper desires should be cultivated, not killed.

The proper antidote for anxiety is *the outpouring of the heart to God.* Here questions occur:

a. *In connection with what situations or circumstances should this take place?*

Answer: "in everything." Note the sharp contrast: "*In nothing* be anxious but *in everything* . . . let your petitions be made known before God." Because of the specific context here, *the emphasis* is, nevertheless, on all such circumstances which might otherwise cause one to worry: "Cast all your anxiety upon him, because he cares for you" (I Peter 5:7). The outpouring of the heart to God should, of course, not be *restricted* to this.

> *Sweet hour of prayer, sweet hour of prayer,*
> *That calls me from a world of care,*
> *And bids me at my Father's throne*
> *Make all my wants and wishes known!*
>
> (W. W. Walford)

b. *In what frame of mind should this be done?*

Answer: *with reverence and true devotion.* That is implied in the words, "by prayer." *Prayer* is any form of reverent address directed to God.

c. *What is the nature of this activity?*

Answer: *it amounts to supplication.* Note: "and supplication." By this is meant the humble cry for the fulfilment of needs that are keenly felt.

d. *What is the condition of acceptance?*

Answer: that this be done "with thanksgiving." This implies humility, submission to God's will, knowing that this will is always best. There must be grateful acknowledgement for: a. past favors, b. present blessings, and c. firmly-grounded assurances for the future. Paul begins nearly every one of his epistles with an outpouring of thanksgiving to God. Throughout his writings he again and again insists on the necessity of giving thanks (Rom. 1:21; 14:6; II Cor. 1:11; 4:15; 9:11, 12; Eph. 5:20; Col. 3:15; etc.). Prayer without thanksgiving is like a bird without wings: such a prayer cannot rise to heaven, can find no acceptance with God.

e. *What are the contents?*

Answer: not vague generalities. The prayer, "Lord, bless all that awaiteth thy blessing" may be proper at times but can be overdone. It is easy to resort to it when one has nothing definite to ask. Paul says, "Let your *petitions* be made known before God." There must be *definite, specific requests* (I John 5:15). That is also clear from the example given us in what is commonly called "The Lord's Prayer" (Matt. 6:9-13). Note also the preposition *before,* in "before God."

One enters into the very presence of God, realizing that nothing is too great for his power to accomplish nor too small for his love to be concerned about. Is he not our Father who in Christ loves us with an infinite love?

4:7

B. The Result

7. Now if joy in the Lord reigns *within* the heart, if magnanimity is shown *all around* to everybody with whom one comes into contact, and if there be constant prayer to God *above,* the result will be *peace.* Paul begins the next sentence by saying, **And the peace of God that surpasses all understanding.** This sweet peace originates in God who himself possesses it in his own being. He is glad to impart it to his children. It is, therefore, "the gift of God's love." He not only gives it; he also maintains it at every step. Hence, it has every right to be called "the peace *of God.*" It is founded on grace. It is merited for believers by Christ (see John 14:27; 16:33; 20:19, 21, 26). Paul speaks of this peace in every one of his letters, often at the opening and at the close, sometimes also in the body of the epistle. In Philippians Paul mentions it, as almost always, immediately after *grace* (in I and II Timothy *mercy* is interposed between *grace* and *peace*). Peace is the smile of God reflected in the soul of the believer. It is the heart's calm after Calvary's storm. It is the firm conviction that he who spared not his own Son will surely also, along with him, freely give us all things (Rom. 8:32). "Thou wilt keep him in perfect peace, whose mind is stayed on thee, because he trusts in thee" (Isa. 26:3). In the present context it is the God-given reward resulting from *joyful* reflection on God's bounties, *magnanimity* toward the neighbor, and trustful *prayer* to God.

This peace *passes all understanding.* With respect to this modifier an interpretation favored by many is this: "God's gift of peace will do far more for us than will any clever planning or calculating on our part. In that sense *peace* surpasses our *understanding.*" Objections, which I share with many, are the following:

(1) This interpretation takes the word *understanding* in a too limited sense.

(2) The parallel, Eph. 3:19, is clear. In that passage the love of Christ is said to surpass knowledge in the sense that, try as they may, believers will never succeed in measuring it in all its breadth, length, height, and depth (Eph. 3:18). Surely, if the passage about Christ's love means that this love is *unfathomable,* why should not the passage about God's *peace* have the same meaning?

By nature man is as totally unable to comprehend this wonderful peace as is a blind man to appreciate a glorious sunset (I Cor. 2:14). And even the believer will never be able fully to grasp the beauty of this Christ-centered gift that surpasses in value all other gifts of God to man. One reason why it is justly esteemed to be very, very precious is that it **will keep guard over your hearts and your thoughts in Christ Jesus.** The Philippians were used to the sight of Roman sentinels standing guard. Thus also, only far more so, God's peace will mount guard at the door of heart and thought. It will prevent carking care from corroding the heart, which is the mainspring of life (Prov. 4:23), the root of thinking (Rom. 1:21), willing (I Cor. 7:37), and feeling (Phil. 1:7). It will also prevent unworthy reasonings from entering thought-life. Thus, if any one should tell the believer that God does not exist and that everlasting life is a mere dream, he would get nowhere, for at that very moment the child of God would be experiencing within himself the realities which the infidel is trying to reason out of existence. The man of trust and prayer has entered that impregnable citadel from which no one can dislodge him; and the name of that fortress is *Christ Jesus* (note: "in Christ Jesus").

Christ's Triumph Over Satan
Colossians 2:15

15. Here follows the last of three important acts whereby God grants to his children the joy of salvation, the three being: (1) forgiveness of sins, (2) the setting aside of the law, and now (3) the disarming of the principalities and authorities. Says Paul: **and having stripped the principalities and the authorities of their power, he publicly exposed them to disgrace by triumphing over them in him.** These "principalities and authorities" are angelic beings, who are here (2:15) pictured as resisting God. It is not exactly clear just why Paul makes mention of them in the present connection. It is possible, nevertheless, that the immediately preceding statement of the abrogation of the law as our *impersonal* accuser may have led to this reference to *personal* accusers, namely, the evil angels. That would certainly be a very natural transition. It also reminds us of the apostle's argumentation in Rom. 8. There, too, having pointed out how the demand of *the law* was satisfied (Rom. 8:1-4), the apostle asks in verse 33, "*Who* shall lay anything to the charge of God's elect?" and in verse 34, "*Who* is he that condemns?" Would anyone say that Paul, well-versed in the Old Testament as he was, did *not* include Satan among those personal accusers? The idea that Satan is the arch-accuser is, indeed, decidedly biblical (Job 1:9-11; Zech. 3:1-5; Rev. 12:10). Of course, the work of Satan and his hosts in their attempt to destroy believers is not confined to that of *accusation.* The baseness of these hordes of evil appears especially in this that first they tempt men to sin, and then, having succeeded in their sinister endeavor, they immediately accuse these same people before God, charging them with those very sins which *they,* these sinister spirits, devised.

Now in the midst of this terrific struggle (cf. Eph. 6:12) the Colossians receive a word of comfort. Says Paul, as it were, You need not be afraid of these hosts of evil, for in principle the battle has already been won. It has been won *for* you. God himself has disarmed these principalities and powers. Did he not rescue us out of the domain of darkness? (Col. 1:13). Is not his Son *the head of every principality and authority?* (Col. 2:10). And is it not true that principalities and authorities (as well as thrones and dominions) are but creatures, having been created in him, through him, and with a view to him? (Col. 1:16). Remember, therefore, that, by means of that same Son, God stripped these principalities and authorities of their power. He utterly disarmed them. Did not Christ triumph over them in the desert of temptation? (Matt. 4:1-11). Did he not bind the strong man (Matt. 12:29), casting out demons again and again to prove it? Did he not see Satan fallen as lightning from heaven? (Luke 10:18). When the devil and his hosts asserted themselves from Gethsemane to Golgotha (Luke 22:3, 53; cf. Ps. 22:12, 16), did not Christ by his vicarious death deprive Satan of even a semblance of legal ground on which to base his accusations? Was not *the accuser of the brothers* cast down, and this not only by means of Christ's vicarious death but also by his triumphant resurrection, ascension, and coronation? (Rev. 12:10; Eph. 1:20-23). Is it not true, then, that by these great redemptive acts God publicly exposed these evil powers to disgrace, leading them captive in triumph, chained, as it were, to his triumphal chariot? Yes, in and through this Son of his love, this triumphant Christ, God has achieved the victory over Satan and all his hosts. And that victory is *your* life and *your* joy. Whatever you need is in Christ.

Psalms, Hymns and Spiritual Songs
Colossians 3.16

There is something else that should also be done if the word of Christ is to dwell among the Colossians richly. It is stated in these words: **(and) by means of psalms, hymns, and spiritual songs singing to God in a thankful spirit, with all your heart.**

Paul clearly recognizes the edifying nature of God-glorifying singing. As to the meaning of the terms *psalms, hymns,* and *spiritual songs* (see also Eph. 5:19) a little investigation quickly shows that it may not be easy to distinguish *sharply* between these three. It is possible that there is here some overlapping of meanings. Thus, in connection with *psalms* it is natural to think of the Old Testament Psalter, and, in support of this view, to appeal to Luke 20:42; 24:44; Acts 1:20; 13:33. So far there is no difficulty. However, expositors are by no means agreed that this can also be the meaning of the word *psalm* in I Cor. 14:26 ("When you assemble, each one has a psalm").

As to *hymns,* in the New Testament the word *hymn* is found only in our present passage (Col. 3:16) and in Eph. 5:19. Augustine, in more than one place, states that a hymn has three essentials: it must be sung; it must be praise; it must be to God. According to this definition it would be possible for an Old Testament psalm, sung in praise to God, to be also a hymn. Thus when Jesus and his disciples were about to leave the Upper Room in order to go to the Mount of Olives, they "hymned" (Matt. 26:30; Mark 14:26). It is held by many that what they hymned was Psalm 115-118. According to Acts 16:25 in the Philippian prison Paul and Silas were *hymning* to God. Is it not altogether probable that some, if not all, of these *hymns* were *psalms*?

Cf. also Heb. 2:12. But if Augustine's definition is correct there are also hymns that do not belong to the Old Testament Psalter; such hymns as the *Magnificat* (Luke 1:46-55) and the *Benedictus* (Luke 1:68-79). Fragments of other New Testament hymns seem to be embedded in the letters of Paul (Eph. 5:14; Col. 1:15-20; I Tim. 3:16, and perhaps others).

The word *song* or *ode* (in the sense of poem intended to be sung) occurs not only in Eph. 5:19 and Col. 3:16 but also in Rev. 5:9; 14:3, where "the new song" is indicated, and in Rev. 15:3, where the reference is to "the song of Moses, the servant of God, and the song of the Lamb." These are not Old Testament Psalms. Moreover, a song or ode is not necessarily a *sacred* song. In the present case the fact that it is, indeed, sacred is shown by the addition of the adjective *spiritual.*

All in all, then, it would seem that when here in Col. 3:16 the apostle uses these three terms, apparently distinguishing them at least to some extent, the term *psalms* has reference, at least mainly, to the Old Testament Psalter; *hymns* mainly to New Testament songs of praise to God or to Christ; and *spiritual songs* mainly to any other sacred songs dwelling on themes other than direct praise to God or to Christ.

The point that must not be ignored is this, that these songs must be sung in a thankful spirit. The songs must be poured forth sincerely, rising from within the humbly grateful hearts of believers. It has been said that next to Scripture itself a good Psalter-Hymnal is the richest fountain of edification. Not only are its songs a source of daily nourishment for the church, but they also serve as a very effective vehicle for the outpouring of confession of sin, gratitude, spiritual joy, rapture. Whether sung in the regular worship-service on the Lord's Day, at a midweek meeting, in social gatherings, in connection with family-worship, at a festive occasion, or privately, they are a tonic for the soul and promote the glory of God. They do this because they fix the interest upon the indwelling word of Christ, and carry the attention away from that worldly cacophony by which people with low moral standards are being emotionally overstimulated.

The passage under discussion has often been used in support of this or that theory with respect to what may or may not be sung in the official worship-service. Perhaps it is correct to say that the appeal is justified if one is satisfied with a few broad, general principles; for example, (1) In our services the psalms should not be neglected. (2) As to *hymns,* in the stricter sense of songs of praise, "It is probably true that a larger proportion of the religious poems which are used in public praise should be 'hymns' in the stricter sense. They should be addressed to God. Too many are subjective, not to say sentimental, and express only personal experiences and aspirations which are sometimes lacking in reality" Charles E. Erdman.

For the rest, it is well to bear in mind that Paul's purpose is not to lay down detailed rules and regulations pertaining to ecclesiastical liturgy. He is interested in showing the Colossians and all those to whom or by whom the letter would be read how they may grow in grace, and may manifest rightly the power of the indwelling word. His admonition, therefore, can be applied to every type of Christian gathering, whether on the Sabbath or during the week, whether in church or at home or anywhere else.

The Events of Christ's Return
I Thessalonians 4.16-18

16, 17. For with a shouted command, with a voice of an archangel and with a trumpet of God, the Lord himself will descend from heaven, and the dead in Christ will rise first; then we who are alive,

who are left, shall be caught up together with them in clouds to meet the Lord in the air.

By separating these two verses – 16 and 17 – many readers have failed to see the true meaning. By printing and reading them together we see at once that here are the same two groups of believers who appear in verse 15. One might present this graphically as follows:

Verse 15	Verses 16, 17
"we, those who remain alive, who are left until the coming of the Lord"	"we who are alive, who are left"
"those who fell asleep"	"the dead in Christ"

It is clear also that both groups – the survivors and the dead (or those fallen asleep) – are *believers*. Anyone can see at once that the apostle is not drawing a contrast between believers and unbelievers, as if, for example, believers would rise first, and unbelievers a thousand years later. He states:

"And *the dead* in Christ will rise first; then *we who are alive, who are left* shall be caught up together with them in clouds . . ."

Both groups ascend to meet the Lord. *Both* consist of nothing but believers.

The various elements in this vivid description of Christ's descent and the rapture of the saints are as follows:

a. *With a shouted command.*

This is the first of *three* phrases showing the *two* circumstances that will attend the Lord's glorious return. He returns as Conqueror. The *shouted command* in the New Testament occurring only here is originally the order which an officer shouts to his troops, a hunter to his dogs, a charioteer to his horses, or a ship-master to his rowers. In the present connection it is clearly the command of the Lord, as he leaves heaven, for the dead to arise. Note the context: those who have fallen asleep shall not be at a disadvantage (verse 15), *for* with a *shout* . . . the Lord himself will descend from heaven, *and the dead in Christ will rise* . . . (verse 16). Just as even here and now the voice of the Son of God is life-giving, causing those who are spiritually dead to be quickened, so also when he comes back "all who are in the tombs will hear his voice and will come out." The command, therefore, is definitely *his own*, proceeding from his *lips*. It is not a command issued *to* him, but an order given *by* him. Leaving heaven in his human nature, he utters his voice, and immediately the souls of the redeemed also leave, and are quickly reunited with their bodies, which, thus restored to life, arise gloriously.

b. *With a voice of an archangel and with a trumpet of God.*

These two phrases, united by the conjunction *and,* probably belong together, so that the archangel is represented as sounding God's trumpet. The term *archangel* or chief angel occurs only here and in Jude 9. In the latter passage Michael is the archangel. On Michael see also Rev. 12:7; then Dan. 10:13, 21; 12:1. He is represented as leader of good angels and as defender of God's people. With respect to the question whether Michael is the only archangel Dr. A. Kuyper expressed himself as follows:

"This question cannot be answered, because Scripture says nothing about it. It is possible that Michael is *the* archangel, that is, the *only* archangel, but it is also possible that he is *one of* the archangels (one of the seven angels that stand before God's throne), as in Daniel 10:13 he is called *one of the chief princes,* so that Gabriel as well as Michael might be an archangel." With that opinion we are in hearty agreement. The fact that the article *(the)* is not used here – so that we have translated *"an* archangel" – does not definitely decide the matter. It may indicate that he is one of several, but it is also possible that the term *archangel* was felt to be definite (a proper name, as it were) even without a preceding article. However that may be, one fact at least is well-nigh certain: "a shouted command" and "an archangel's voice" are two different things. The former proceeds from the Christ, the latter from his archangel. Nevertheless, the two sounds have this in common, that they are the signal for the dead to be raised (I Cor. 15:52). (Note that also in Josh. 6:5 and Judg. 7:21, 22 the shout and the trumpet-blast go together.) At the sound of the trumpet the surviving believers are changed, in a moment, in the twinkling of an eye (again I Cor. 15:52).

The trumpet-blast, in this connection, is certainly very fitting. In the old dispensation, when God "came down," as it were, to meet with his people, this meeting was announced by a trumpet-blast (e.g., Ex. 19:16, 17: "and the sound of a trumpet exceeding loud . . . and Moses brought the people out of the camp to meet God"; cf. Ex. 19:19). Hence, when the marriage of the Lamb with his bride reaches its culmination (cf. Rev. 19:7), this trumpet-blast is most appropriate. Also, the trumpet was used as a signal of Jehovah's coming to rescue his people from hostile oppression (Zeph. 1:16; Zech. 9:14). It was the signal for their deliverance. So also this final trumpet-blast, the signal for the dead to arise, for the living to be changed, and for all the elect to be gathered from the four winds (Matt. 24:31) to meet the Lord, may well be interpreted as being also the fulfilment of the trumpet-ordinance found in Lev. 25, and, accordingly, as proclaiming liberty throughout the universe for all the children of God, their everlasting jubilee!

From all this it becomes abundantly clear that the Lord's coming will be open, public, not only visible but also audible. There are, indeed, interpreters, who, in view of the fact that the Bible at times employs figurative language, take the position that we can know nothing about these eschatological events. To them these precious paragraphs in which the Holy Spirit reveals the future convey no meaning at all. But this is absurd. Scripture was written to be understood, and when it tells us that the Lord will descend from heaven with a shout, with a voice of an archangel and a trumpet of God, it certainly must mean at least this: that in addition to the shouted command of our Lord (which might be compared with John 11:43), a reverberating sound will actually pervade the universe. What forces of nature will be employed to produce this sound has not been revealed. One fact has now become evident: for believers this sound will be full of cheer. This is *God's* trumpet! It is *his* signal, for the archangel is *his* angel. It is sounded to proclaim *his* deliverance for *his* people. Cf. Rev. 15:2 ("harps *of God*"). It announces the coming of *his* Son (as "Lord of lords and King of kings," Rev. 19:16) for the deliverance of *his* people!

   c. *The Lord himself* (or *he, the Lord*) *will descend from heaven.*

   This descent is visible (Rev. 1:7), audible (as has just been shown), majestic, unto judgment and deliverance (Matt. 25:31-46). If the words, "He shall so come in like manner as you beheld him going into heaven" may be interpreted somewhat broadly, it would seem that the actual *descent* (as distinguished now from the suddenness and unexpectedness of Christ's appearance, and from the suddenness and finality that characterizes the entire return) will be character-ized by a kind of majestic leisureliness. Note the description of the ascension in Acts 1:9, 10. At any rate, it will not be an *instantaneous* change of location from heaven to earth. There will be time (Rev. 10:6, correctly interpreted, is not in conflict with this) for the souls of those who had fallen asleep to leave their heavenly abodes, to be reunited with their bodies, and then in these gloriously raised bodies to ascend to meet the Lord in the air!

   d. *And the dead in Christ will rise first.*

   See what has been said about this in the preceding. The meaning here is very clearly that those who departed from this life in Christ, and are here viewed as having remained in Christ, shall not be at a disadvantage. They will rise before the believers who survive on earth will ascend to meet the Lord. The survivors will have to wait a moment, as it were.

   e. *Then we who are alive, who are left, shall be caught up together with them in clouds to meet the Lord in the air.*

   In addition to what has already been said, note the following: the fact that Paul says *we* does not necessarily mean that he expected to be among those who would still be living at Christ's return. He says *we* because right now he, Silas, Timothy, the readers, are among those believers still living on earth. He immediately modifies this by interpreting it to mean: "those who are left (when the Lord comes)," in order to indicate that only God knows who they may be. Paul knows that the second coming will not take place immediately (see II Thess. 2:2); and while he was in Thessalonica, this element in his teaching regarding the last things was not neglected (II Thess. 2:5). Moreover, the saying of Jesus recorded in Matt. 24:36 was certainly not unknown to Paul. Of course, it is also true that Paul never taught that the Lord would definitely not come during this apostle's life-time. He probably hoped that he might live to see it. He wanted everyone to conduct himself in such a manner as to be always ready. But he does not set any date.

Note: *we, together with them*. There is complete impartiality: survivors have no advantage. The predicate is *shall be caught up* (cf. for the verb also Acts 8:39 – Philip the evangelist was caught away by the Spirit of the Lord; II Cor. 12:2-4 – a man in Christ was caught up to the third heaven; and Rev. 12:5 – the Christ-child is caught up, snatched away, from the power of the dragon).

The suddenness, the swiftness, and the divine character of the power which is operative in this *being snatched up* are here emphasized. The survivors have been changed "in a moment, in the twinkling of an eye" (I Cor. 15:52). The heavens and the earth, in their present form, are *put to flight* (Rev. 20:11; cf. 6:14). Now while figurative language abounds in this vivid description, one fact remains: the dramatic suddenness and swiftness of the series of events is stressed. Once the Lord appears upon the clouds of heaven and begins to descend, there will be no opportunity for conversion. His coming is absolutely decisive. He comes not to convert but to judge. (See also II Thess. 2:8; cf. Matt. 25:31 ff; II Cor. 6:2; and II Peter 3:9.) *Now* is the acceptable time; *now is* the day of salvation.

The raised and the changed are caught up together *in clouds to meet the Lord in the air*. Although these clouds may well be taken literally, nevertheless, they also have a symbolical meaning. They are associated with the coming of the Lord in majesty, for the punishment of the enemies of his saints, hence for the salvation of his people (cf. Dan. 7:13; then Matt. 26:64; finally, Ex. 19:16, 20; Ps. 97:2; Nah. 1:3).

According to Moulton and Milligan (p. 53) the expression *to meet* was used in connection with an official welcome accorded to a newly arrived dignitary. No doubt the *welcoming* idea is also included in the expression as used here in I Thess. 4:17. That all believers, the raised as well as (and together with) the changed, shall ascend to meet the Lord *in the air is* clearly taught here. Whether such passages as Job 19:25; Acts 1:11 actually teach that *the judgment is* going to take place *on earth* is debatable. At any rate, nothing with respect to this is taught in the present passage. However, the main thrust of I Thess. 4:17 is not that we shall meet the Lord *in the air,* but that all believers together shall *meet the Lord, never to be separated from him:*

18. And so shall we always be with the Lord. Therefore encourage one another with these words. In these words is stated the conclusion of the entire paragraph. Since it has become clear that those who fell asleep in Christ are not at a disadvantage as compared with those who survive, there is solid ground for encouragement. Naturally such encouragement is meant not only for the close relatives of bereaved ones, but for all. It must be borne in mind that the members of this very young church were closely united by the bond of love. Hence, when *one* sorrowed, *all* sorrowed; when *one* rejoiced, *all* rejoiced. The encouragement, then, is for all. The members must encourage *one another.*

New Testament Commentaries
by William Hendriksen

available in the UK from Banner of Truth Trust
(www.banneroftruth.co.uk)

Matthew, ISBN 978085151 1924

Mark, ISBN 978085151 2327

Luke, ISBN 978085151 2921

John, ISBN 978085151 1061

Romans, ISBN 978085151 3652

Galatians & Ephesians, ISBN 978085151 3331

Philippians, Colossians & Philemon, ISBN 978085151 4550

Thessalonians, Timothy & Titus, ISBN 978085151 3850

The Bible on the Life Hereafter
William Hendriksen

222 pages, paperback, Wakeman Great Reprints, ISBN 978 1 870855 51 8

The very best short book on the afterlife, Heaven, the Lord's return, and all related issues. It consists of numerous three or four-page chapters, each answering a common question such as, 'Shall we know one another in Heaven?' and, 'What is the millennium?' It is ideal also for giving to bereaved Christians.

Included is the most superb explanation of *Revelation 20* to be found. This is a 'model' in communication from a master of the craft!

Israel in Prophecy
William Hendriksen

63 pages, paperback, Wakeman Great Reprints, ISBN 978 1 870855 52 5

For many years now this little book has been gold dust, being both rare and precious. Originally penned in the 1950s it presents the outstanding commentator's answers to some of the most important questions for Bible students, namely:

Are the 'restoration of the Jews' promises being fulfilled today?
Is God finished with the Jews?
What is meant by Israel?
Are the blessings promised to Israel for the Jews or for the Church?

No other book gives the answers so plainly and scripturally as this, for Dr Hendriksen was truly a master of brief and crystal-clear reasoning. He shows that the promises of the Old Testament apply ultimately to the Church, but counsels understanding, appreciation and soul-winning zeal toward the Jews.

Physicians of Souls
The Gospel Ministry
Peter Masters

285 pages, paperback, ISBN 978 1 870855 34 1

'Compelling, convicting, persuasive preaching, revealing God's mercy and redemption to dying souls, is seldom heard today. The noblest art ever granted to our fallen human race has almost disappeared.'

Even where the free offer of the Gospel is treasured in principle, regular evangelistic preaching has become a rarity, contends the author. These pages tackle the inhibitions, theological and practical, and provide powerful encouragement for physicians of souls to preach the Gospel. A vital anatomy or order of conversion is supplied with advice for counselling seekers.

The author shows how passages for evangelistic persuasion may be selected and prepared. He also challenges modern church growth techniques, showing the superiority of direct proclamation. These and other key topics make up a complete guide to soul-winning.

Worship in the Melting Pot
Peter Masters

148 pages, paperback, ISBN 978 1 870855 33 4

'Worship is truly in the melting pot,' says the author. 'A new style of praise has swept into evangelical life shaking to the foundations traditional concepts and attitudes.' How should we react? Is it all just a matter of taste and age? Will churches be helped, or changed beyond recognition?

This book presents four essential principles which Jesus Christ laid down for worship, and by which every new idea must be judged.

Here also is a fascinating view of how they worshipped in Bible times, including their rules for the use of instruments, and the question is answered – What does the Bible teach about the content and order of a service of worship today?

Not Like Any Other Book
Peter Masters
161 pages, paperback, ISBN 978 1 870855 43 3

Faulty Bible interpretation lies at the root of every major mistake and 'ism' assailing churches today, and countless Christians are asking for the old, traditional and proven way of handling the Bible to be spelled out plainly.

A new approach to interpretation has also gripped many evangelical seminaries and Bible colleges, an approach based on the ideas of unbelieving critics, stripping the Bible of God's message, and leaving pastors impoverished in their preaching.

This book reveals what is happening, providing many brief examples of right and wrong interpretation. The author shows that the Bible includes its own rules of interpretation, and every believer should know what these are.

Faith, Doubts, Trials and Assurance
Peter Masters
139 pages, paperback, ISBN 978 1 870855 50 1

Ongoing faith is essential for answered prayer, effective service, spiritual stability and real communion with God. In this book many questions are answered about faith, such as –

How may we assess the state of our faith? How can faith be strengthened? What are the most dangerous doubts? How should difficult doubts be handled? What is the biblical attitude to trials? How can we tell if troubles are intended to chastise or to refine? What can be done to obtain assurance? What are the sources of assurance? Can a believer commit the unpardonable sin? Exactly how is the Lord's presence felt?

Dr Masters provides answers, with much pastoral advice, drawing on Scripture throughout.

For other Wakeman titles please see: www.wakemantrust.org